The Creator's Canvas

Stephen Payne

May the Lord bless you!
Stephen Payne

Diakonia Publishing
USA

ISBN-13: 978-0-9800877-0-3
ISBN-10: 0-9800877-0-8
Library of Congress Catalog Number: 2007943957

First edition.

Published by Diakonia Publishing
P.O. Box 9512
Greensboro, North Carolina 27429-0512
Visit our web site: www.ephesians412.net

Table of Contents

To Daniel Faubion

…who not only inspired in me a love for the mountains,
but who also introduced me to their Creator.
I love you, brother.

Introduction

For as long as I can remember, I've always loved the outdoors. Surrounded by the city, my youthful mind would spend hours contemplating my next escape. As soon as Saturday rolled around, I would hop on my bike, armed with a sack lunch and a fishing pole, and head for the hills. When the interminable wait for summer was finally over, I closed my high school locker for the last time, the chains fell off, and I was free to head up to the high Sierra. That was about as close as I could imagine to heaven on earth.

My love of the creation preceded my love for the Creator. Then at age seventeen, when I was working as an assistant guide for Sierra Mountaineering Experience, Dan Faubion, the head guide, introduced me to the One who was responsible for the majesty that awed me. After telling me he had been praying for me since the previous summer, Dan asked me to read the book of John in the Bible. So for the first time I read about a man who was called the Word, who by his word had brought all things into existence, one who was really much more than just a man. I had never heard of Jesus before, except as a swear word, but as I read about his life, God answered the prayers of my friend. A light went on inside and I surrendered my life to the One who had surrendered his life for me.

Knowing the Creator didn't diminish my love for the outdoors; rather, it put a new song in my heart. What before was simply a yodel of joy when topping a new ridge became a shout of praise to the One who had created the scene before me. I loved hiking and fishing and I soon added to those a love of rock climbing, then cross-country skiing, then alpine climbing. The steeper and higher the slope, the more I enjoyed it.

My interest in photography paralleled my interest in the outdoors. My Pentax K1000 was by no means light, but everywhere I went it earned a place in my pack. Back in those early days all I had was a 50mm lens. Looking back through those first boxes of slides, I'm still amazed at all the scenes captured by that one simple lens.

As I grew in faith I started to identify more and more with the statement by C.T. Studd, "One life to live that soon will pass, only what's done for Christ will last." I read that saying written over a door in Bolivia, where I had gone on a short-term missions trip. The trip confirmed my sense of calling to a life of mission work, so I returned to the States for Bible College and then for training in Wycliffe Bible Translator's linguistics program where I met my wife Laura. Once Laura and I finished the training program, we raised our support to go overseas; our destination was (of course) Nepal. It was extremely difficult to get into Nepal in the late 1980s, but Laura had the possibility of using her teaching credential to provide us with a visa, and I was then hoping to work full time on Bible translation. After all the reading I had done of climbing excursions to the Himalayas, I was primarily interested in the Sherpa people, who were without a Bible in their language.

However, at the last minute, the teaching position in Nepal fell through, and we had no other hope of obtaining a visa. There were no other countries with mountains in Wycliffe's "Urgent Need" category, so Laura and I looked at where else God might be able to use us. We ended up in Senegal, W. Africa, a country with nary a mountain at all. Retiring my climbing rope and crampons was perhaps the biggest sacrifice I had ever made, but I was willing to go wherever my Lord would lead me in order to reach the lost. And Senegal was definitely a needy land spiritually, with more than 92% of the population Muslim, and less than 0.01% evangelical Christian. For the next ten years we lived in a remote village without electricity or running water, translating the New Testament for the Kwatay people. There I learned that God had not just used nature to create a beautiful canvas, but that people were part of his creative work as well. There were not many beautiful landscapes for my camera to capture in Senegal, but the smile of a child here, or the laugh of an old woman there, shone like jewels through the backdrop of poverty.

After many years overseas, we returned to the States for our children's high school education. I continue to make trips to Africa to train nationals in Bible translation, but our base is currently in the hill country of Southern Oregon. Now, once again, I find I'm able to plan my next escape to the mountains. It may take the form of a quick afternoon hike after work, a Saturday kayak down the Rogue River, a day of cross-country skiing up at Crater Lake, a weekend climb of Mt. Shasta, or, for my vacation time, a summer backpack in the high Sierra. God has allowed me another opportunity to explore the alpine world, and it is there that I see the beauty of creation in its purest form.

It has often been said, "Beauty is in the eye of the beholder." While there is a kernel of truth in the old cliché, still, the appreciation of beauty is not wholly an individual matter. We all appreciate some things as beautiful. The photos chosen for a calendar or a postcard are generally ones we all consider to be striking. Those who enter Yosemite Valley for the first time, or who approach the snow-clad Tetons, or who take in the panorama from the rim above Crater Lake, know they have seen something majestic. Each time we see the golden colors of a sunset as the sun sinks into the ocean we are unanimous in describing it as beautiful. God has made everything, but there are certain scenes that elicit a visceral response. Capturing those through a lens is the nature photographer's challenge.

I love both writing and photography. A writer is a sculptor whose medium is paper. He chips off a few words here; he carves a new paragraph there. The work slowly takes form amidst frequent polishings. The photographer is an artist as well. The tools of his trade – historically the

negative and the enlarger – have given way to more modern apparatus: the digital camera and Photoshop. The photographer also chips and carves and polishes. Sometimes this is done before the picture is taken, through adding filters or adjusting the aperture or shutter speed. Other times it is done in post processing, adjusting levels and sharpness and contrast. Whereas Ansel Adams would spend days or weeks in the darkroom, laboriously making hundreds of prints of the same image before finally getting one to match the image he had in his mind, the modern photographer can use sliders in a computer program to immediately visualize the effects of changed settings.

While painting and sculpting are classically defined as art, it has long been debated whether photography is an art form. The vast majority of camera owners take photos to record an event or preserve a memory. Their snapshots of friends and birthdays and vacations fill family photo albums. But others seek something more with their cameras. They will adjust the aperture and white balance, or spend hours waiting for just the right light to illuminate their subject. They will climb high or stoop low to find just the right vantage point for the angle they want to capture in their composition.

For many, art means composing something where nothing existed before. The painter applies his brush to a blank canvas, and something of beauty appears. A musician puts notes together in a unique sequence to compose a new melody. A poet takes ordinary words and combines them in an extraordinary way to create a written work of art. Some might argue that the photographer does not start with a blank page; he merely captures what already exists. But he, too, starts with a blank roll of unexposed film – or a blank memory card. In the same way the musician uses pre-existing notes or the poet uses pre-existing words, the photographer uses pre-existing light and images to create his composition. The number of possible angles and the permutations of lighting are infinite. The choices the photographer makes determine whether or not his work will grace the wall of a gallery, be relegated to the family photo album, or worse!

Though a painter must draw on his understanding of the natural world, when God created the heavens and the earth, he truly created something from nothing. God is therefore the true Master Painter, the Supreme Artist. We do not often consider nature to be a work of art, perhaps because it is so vast. But God has big hands, and his canvas is equally large!

This book traces God's work as he created the heavens and the earth. After six days of creative activity, God then took a day of rest. We, too, would do well to follow his example, to rest and contemplate all that has been made for our benefit, and praise the One who made it.

Wherever we look, it does not take long to see the Creator's imprint. From the most powerful telescope to the most powerful microscope, symmetry and patterns are immediately apparent, providing visual evidence of the Designer's activity. After creating the heavens and the earth, God declared that "everything that he had made … was *very* good" (Genesis 1:31). My purpose in writing this book is to help us see anew all that God had made, and to come to the conclusion that not only is his handiwork good, but so also is the One who accomplished it. He is worthy of our praise not only for what he has done, but for who he is.

The Six Days of Creation

It is difficult to visualize how the universe appeared the first few days when God was at work. On the first day he makes light, separating it from the darkness. Our idea of light is so closely linked with the sun, moon and stars that it's hard for us to imagine what we might have seen if we could go back and look at the result of God's first day of work.

The second day is also a bit hard to fathom. On this day God separates the waters above from the waters below. What the world was like before this separation occurred is beyond our comprehending, but the result afterward was, on the one hand, air, sky and atmosphere, and on the other an endless sea, covering the whole earth. At this point in the story of creation, the earth seems cold and inhospitable, but all the basic building blocks of life are now in place: just the right mixture of oxygen and nitrogen, water in abundance, and all the other essential elements necessary to sustain life.

On day three, the world starts to look more like we know it today. The waters below are gathered to one place, and thus are born mountains, valleys, plains, beaches, lakes and rivers. What a transformation! But God does not end his work there. He speaks a second time on day three and another transformation takes place. The newly formed land is now filled with vegetation: every kind of tree, plant, flower and grass – a garden of greenery! No longer is the world flat and watery; now there is topography teeming with the first forms of life.

At the start of day four, God is halfway through his creative work, and once again he turns his attention to creating light. He hangs in the sky both a light producer and a light reflector. He then starts the earth spinning on its axis so that its inhabitants will have a never-ending cycle of light and darkness. And then he spins the earth around the sun, giving us spring and summer, fall and winter. Almost as an afterthought, the Scriptures record that God also creates the stars – billions of galaxies, numbers which boggle the mind, but which also help us gain an inkling of how big our God really is.

On the fifth day God returns his attention to filling the earth with various life forms. The trees and flowers he created on day three are alive, but on this day he creates living beings which move and breathe. And so a myriad of creatures fills the sea and another myriad wings their way across the sky. The twittering of birds fills the air with song, while the deep is broken by the melodies of the humpback whale.

Day six is God's final day of work before declaring his creation complete. On this day he fills the land with all kinds of animals – some that run, others that slither, still others that hop. Everything he has created up until this point is "good" – but there is still something missing. God has saved the best for last! He decides to make a creature in his very own image. A creature who would think and choose and relate. A creature who would love. And so God creates man and he creates woman. They are the last thing he creates. He is done. The Creator's canvas is complete. And now it is not just "good," it is "very good." Very good indeed!

On day seven God rests. He doesn't make anything at all. He just sits back and enjoys all that he has made. He sets an example for us to follow, knowing how tempted we are to tirelessly pursue our own creations. And so day seven is set aside as a Sabbath, a day to remember all that God has made, and a day to adore him for who he is. The seventh day is not a day for making new creations, but a day for sitting back and reflecting on the Creator's canvas. If we do, it's a day that is sure to be filled with praise.

Light – Day One of Creation

God called the light "day," and the darkness he called "night."
…And there was evening, and there was morning – the first day.   Genesis 1:3-5

My favorite place on earth is the Sierra Nevada, which John Muir so aptly called "the Range of Light." It is an outdoor cathedral, a veritable playground of light. Without a range of light, we wouldn't be able to distinguish the mountains from the sky, the needles from a fir tree, the petals from a wildflower. The first time God speaks, as recorded in the Scriptures, he says, "Let there be light." (Genesis 1:3). And all the various shades and hues came into being. Just as he created an almost infinite number of life forms on subsequent days, on this first day of creation God created an almost infinite variety of shades of light. The human eye is capable of distinguishing about ten million different colors. The camera lens goes even further and picks up the infrared range which our eyes miss, but there are many other shades to which both we and the camera are oblivious. God could have created just a handful of wavelengths, but instead he chose to bless his creation with tremendous variety. So we are the recipients of the various reds and yellows, greens and blues. We've named the colors just as we named the animals, but our words do scant justice to what our eyes behold. The changing alpenglow in the high Sierra changes minute by minute from a rosy hue to a bold red to a deep magenta, but my eyes register the millions of other shades my mouth cannot name.

God did himself proud on that first day! He didn't just create one thing – light – and then decide it was time for a rest. He created a myriad of lights, a whole spectrum of color. Why was it important to him to do this? I believe it was in order to give his last creation, man, the ability to glimpse the intricacy of his handiwork. Our eyes drink in the greens of the meadow swathed in sunlight, the aquamarine of a tropical cove, the explosion of colors as the sun ends its daily journey across the heavens. It is light which allows us to truly appreciate the Creator's canvas.

One thing I really enjoy is sleeping on top of a mountain. It's a lot of work carrying up sleeping gear, cooking gear, and sufficient water, but the sweeping panoramas and the magnificence of the sunset and sunrise make every grueling step worth it. As every nature photographer knows, horizontal light is the most flattering to a subject. Consequently the hour before sunset and the hour after sunrise are prime photo times. Those are also meal times, so the photographer must often choose between his breakfast or dinner and a chance at a better-than-mediocre photo.

> Light gives God's last creation, man, the ability to glimpse the intricacy of his handiwork

The Scriptures say that God lives in *unapproachable* light. Perhaps the only glimpse we humans have of what that really means is that we are unable to look directly at the sun. Even though it is 93 million miles away, the sun is too bright, too powerful to behold directly. And so it is with God, though his brightness far outshines the sun. No wonder no one can see God and live. No wonder man, in his present untransformed state, isn't able to enter into God's presence, much as he says he longs to do that very thing.

At times I wonder what the light of heaven will be like. Will the heavenly spectrum be broader, the colors more deeply saturated? The apostle John, in his vision of heaven, tells us that there will be no darkness, no night, and no sun, for God himself will be our light. Our eyes will no longer see sunlight, but "Godlight," a light which, I imagine, would render our present high definition screens, with their "billions of colors," woefully inadequate. John attempts to use color in his description of God in the heavenly Jerusalem, but seems somewhat at a loss for words. So he employs similes and metaphorical language: "His head and hair were white like wool … his eyes were like flaming fire … his feet were like bronze … his face was like the sun shining in all its brilliance" (Revelation 20:14-16). As amazing as it might seem, we now see only dimly, as through a dirty piece of glass.

Usually I'm enthralled by the colors I see as I look through the viewfinder of my camera. But if I could somehow capture a few images of a God-lit scene, it would make my present photos seem as though they were totally bereft of color. The Scriptures say, "No eye has seen, no ear has heard, no mind has conceived what God has prepared for those who love him" (1 Corinthians 2:9). For God to prepare the present heavens and earth took six days. Compare that with over 700,000 days (two thousand years) since Jesus said, "I am going to prepare a place for you … that you also may be where I am" (John 14:2). Indeed, we cannot even imagine what it will be like to approach the unapproachable and to see the invisible. All we know for sure is that in the presence of God all will be glorious.

As a photographer, I can't help but wonder whether or not I will still want to take photos when I get to heaven. I think I probably will. I think I'll still have the same desire to record, appreciate, and share God's handiwork. However, when the long-awaited day finally arrives and all I see is lit by a wonderful, new light emanating directly from God, I think I'll be in need of a new camera!

"Everything exposed by the light becomes visible, for it is light that makes everything visible."   *(Ephesians 5:13-14)*

"God is light; in him there is no darkness at all." *(John 1:5)*

"God alone is immortal and lives in unapproachable light, no one has seen him or can see him." *(1 Timothy 6:16)*

"A single sunbeam is enough to drive away many shadows."   *St. Francis of Assisi*

"Photographs recreate for me, moods, realities and magical experiences…" *Ansel Adams*

"The darkness is passing and the true light is already shining."   *(1 John 2:8)*

Interaction with the Creator – The Brightest Light

The brightest light I've ever seen lasted for only a fraction of a second. It came down from the sky in a bolt of living power, and hit a granite boulder about 75 feet in front of me. The shock wave of sound was instantaneous, causing small pieces of gravel next to the boulder to fly into the air. A smell akin to burning sulfur filled my nostrils.

The late afternoon sky over the high Sierra was turbulent, but no rain had yet fallen. We'd been hearing distant thunder for five to ten minutes, but had not realized the storm was moving our way. The bolt caught us by surprise as we crossed an exposed ridge above timberline. I thought of my ice axe a foot or so behind my head, sticking up above my backpack. It could easily have attracted the last lightning bolt, and it could just as easily attract the next one. There were twelve of us in the group, spread out along the trail, and we all gathered together amidst animated exclamations of, "Did you see that?" and "Can you believe it?" We stayed the next ten minutes or so in a low area off to the side of the ridge as the wind picked up and scattered raindrops began to fall. The booming thunder soon became distant again, and we shouldered our packs and scurried off to set up our tarps and get out of the rain.

Since that day I've read Bob Madgic's account in his book *Shattered Air* of the five people who were injured or killed in Yosemite by a lightning storm on Half Dome. The gravity of our own situation largely passed me by that summer afternoon in the Sierras. God was gracious though, and kept our group from harm.

I've seen one other extremely bright light in my life, but it was not with my eyes. I saw it rather in a dream – a dream so amazing that as I woke up from it right at the high point I was absolutely filled to overflowing with an incredible sense of rapture.

I was probably 18 or 19 years old when I had the dream, and I had only recently become a Christian. In the dream I was in a cathedral with a high peaked roof and there was a big stained glass window over tall doors at the entrance of the sanctuary. As I walked down the center aisle toward the doors, suddenly, with no effort of my own, I started moving faster. I walked, yet my feet no longer hit the flagstones. I was walking on air! Light was streaming through the stained glass window. As I went

through the doors, I rose faster and faster, over the courtyard and the large grassy plaza. Before me were clouds and a brilliant white light. I awoke as I ascended into the light. My chest was tight with a feeling of incredible joy. What a dream!

I didn't meet my wife Laura until a number of years later, and I didn't tell her of the dream until almost ten years after that. Amazingly, she had once had a dream in which she too was raptured and met Christ in the air. As we compared what we remembered of the dreams, the details were very similar. It was as if we were both in the same place when it happened!

Since that day we keep our eyes open for the place we saw in our dreams. We don't go around specifically looking for it, thinking that we can in any way speed the coming of the Lord. But when it happens, we'll be ready! We got a little taste of what it will be like to enter the Lord's presence and to be filled with the joy of the Spirit. We long for the day when we will once again see that heavenly light.

Sky – Day Two of Creation

God called the expanse "sky." ...And there was evening, and there was morning – the second day. Genesis 1:6-8

We often take the sky for granted, but really it's an amazing thing! Oxygen, nitrogen and carbon dioxide are invisible to the naked eye, yet they are essential to life as we know it. Not only did God give our planet just the right amount of each (78% nitrogen, 21% oxygen, 0.03% carbon dioxide), but he also established a system that continually maintains the correct balance. Both man and animals breathe in oxygen and breathe out carbon dioxide. Plants and trees use carbon dioxide in the process of photosynthesis and produce oxygen. It's a good example of the circle of life, like intertwined cogs of a watch, working together to keep the whole thing ticking, pointing irrevocably to the existence of a master Designer.

Because air is largely invisible, we often forget it is there. Soft breezes are gentle reminders that the unseen is real, while hurricanes and tornadoes drive home the fact with terrifying aplomb. Jesus said that the wind is an image of God's Spirit (John 3:8). God, who like the wind is also unseen, is nevertheless real, and his acts can be seen and felt by those whose eyes are open to his working.

In my work as a missionary I've done a fair bit of traveling by airplane. Even though I've studied the principles of aerodynamics, it never ceases to amaze me that a 900,000 pound 747 is being held aloft by a bit of air trying to rush in and fill a vacuum. How much air is there at 40,000 feet anyway? And why isn't the vacuum filled with air from above the wing, where there is no metal obstacle to block it? Of course, the physicists can write out long equations to explain how thousands of pounds of metal stay aloft, but the clouds next to the plane seem to defy equations. They do not operate according to the principles of aerodynamics, and yet somehow *billions* of pounds of water droplets float merrily along, waiting for some mysterious sign from God before opening their taps and slowly letting out their stored bounty.

Besides returning water from the oceans to the mountains in another great circle of life, clouds also provide an ever changing visual tapestry of both form and color. Children delight in identifying myriads of shapes as they float by, while adults are mesmerized by endless hues as the setting sun lights the sky in a blaze of crimson glory.

When we ponder what God has made, we are inevitably led to spontaneous praise and expressions of appreciation

Other phenomena also light up the sky, though their appearances are rather infrequent. Lightning streaks down from heaven to earth and occasionally from earth to heaven in cataclysmic displays, accompanied by booming groans as the air is rent in two, superheated to five times the temperature of the sun. Viewing such an apocalyptic display from afar is beautiful, but since it can be terrifying when seen up close, God gave another sign in the sky as a testimony of his eternal love for those he created. So we are comforted by arching bands of refracted light, displaying a rainbow of color.

The psalmist, King David, was once a poor shepherd who watched over his flock by night. Familiar with the night sky, he penned, "The heavens declare the glory of God" (Psalm 19:1). Frederick Lehman wrote a popular hymn which also uses the sky in an attempt to describe God and his love for man. One of the strophes says,

Could we with ink the ocean fill,
And were the skies of parchment made,
Were every stalk on earth a quill,
And every man a scribe by trade,
To write the love of God above,
Would drain the ocean dry.
Nor could the scroll contain the whole,
Though stretched from sky to sky.

Whereas man's photographs and works of art are static, God has a creative medium which is dynamic and ever changing. Each cloud painted on the sky is different from the next! Each of the trillion snowflakes that falls from the sky in a winter storm is different from the next! Every rainbow and every bolt of lightning is different from the next! What is our response when confronted with such diversity, such endless creativity? If we take the time to ponder such things we are inevitably led to spontaneous praise and expressions of appreciation. Yet too often we are the victims of familiarity, and the clouds and snowflakes and air and wind – all that God created on the second day – barely merit a second glance.

Part of my reason in writing such a book is to inspire us to ponder anew the building blocks of life. I want to help us recapture in our minds those moments when we lay on our backs in a grassy meadow and imagined horses and chariots and dragons floating across the heavens. How such frivolity must please the Creator! How it must inspire him as he prepares to once again touch his brush to the canvas! Let us be as children, who look with adoring eyes and wonderment on the accomplishments of our heavenly Father.

"Be exalted, O God, above the highest heavens! May your glory shine over all the earth."   *(Psalm 57:5, NLT)*

"Though we travel the world over to find the beautiful, we must carry it with us or we find it not."   *Ralph Waldo Emerson*

"To the illumined mind the whole world burns and sparkles with light." *Ralph Waldo Emerson*

"Everybody needs beauty as well as bread, places to play in and pray in,
where nature may heal and cheer and give strength to body and soul alike."   *John Muir*

"Climb the mountains and get their good tidings. Nature's peace will flow into you as sunshine flows into trees.
The wind will blow their own freshness into you, and the storms their energy, while cares will drop off like autumn leaves." *John Muir*

"There is no one like the God of Israel. He rides across the heavens to help you, across the skies in majestic splendor."
(Deuteronomy 33:26, NLT)

"He makes the clouds his chariot and rides on the wings of the wind." *(Psalm 104:3)*

"The highest heavens belong to the Lord, but the earth he has given to man."   *(Psalm 115:16)*

Interaction with the Creator – Falling Through the Air

As an artist, God has many wonderful works which elicit a response of appreciation and awe. Often such exhibits are solitary, like the 620-foot Multnomah Falls along the Columbia River Gorge. The waterfall is spectacular, but the next place of interest is several miles distant. Rarely in nature are several works of art displayed in close proximity. Such places seem almost magical. Yosemite Valley is just such a place. The glacially sculpted form of Half Dome, the massive granite face of El Capitan, the twin roars of Upper and Lower Yosemite Falls, the spectacular rainbow mist at Vernal Falls … the list goes on and on. Everywhere you turn is a photographer's paradise, an endearing justification for why Ansel Adams spent so much of his career there.

If one were to try and choose God's *masterpiece* – his greatest piece of creative work – Yosemite Valley would surely come near the top of the list. Yosemite grabbed my heart when I was 17 years old. It was like a siren in Greek mythology, but I simultaneously heard two calls: the first to capture its beauty with my Pentax K1000, and the second to explore its heights with my Five Ten rock shoes. The latter call proved slightly stronger. I had swallowed the rock climbing lure, hook, line and sinker, and life was best when I was facing the challenge of vertical rock. I was fairly new to the sport back in 1979, and after a number

of outings I was excited with the prospect of doing my first wall climb. A wall climb is one that goes from the valley floor all the way to the top. In those days the talk was all about El Capitan. Royal Robbins had climbed "The Captain" back in 1960 in a seven day ascent, but John Long had just completed it in a single day. The sheer north face of Half Dome was another famous climb, usually taking several days, the top overhang being scaled on aid using fixed hardware and etriers. For our first wall, three friends and I decided on Royal Arches, which starts just behind the Ahwahnee Hotel. The climb is 17 pitches, but it's only rated 5.7 and it can be done in a single day. We had two rope teams of two, and we spent a wonderful day scaling the black banded arches. We prided ourselves on seeing new aspects of God's masterpiece which were all but invisible to the thronging crowd of tourists far below.

The 17th pitch at the top of the Royal Arches route is somewhat of a traverse over to the trees, and from there a trail leads up over the top and back around Washington Column to the valley floor. I was on the first rope team and led the pitch. About halfway across, I was met by shiny green moss as a small spring somewhere above trickled water onto the polished granite face. Rather than risk traversing the slick moss, it seemed it would be better to go up and see if

I might find a better place above to cross over to the trees. I wedged a stopper into a crack, clipped my rope into the carabiner and started up. There was nowhere else to place protection, but it wasn't too steep and I wasn't worried. Thirty feet up was a small sloping ledge I could make my way across and be off the route. I had to make one step in the green

moss, but the granite had a few indentations so it looked safe. However, the sticky smooth soles of my rock shoes didn't hold to the moss. Suddenly I found myself hurtling through the air – 30 feet to my last piece of protection, then another 30 – until there was no more slack. The rope caught me at the same time I landed on my rear on a sloping ledge covered with pine needles. The force knocked me out for a minute, but then I heard my climbing partner anxiously calling out to me, "Are you all right?" "Yeah, I'm okay," I mouthed groggily, struggling to form the words. He was around a corner so I couldn't see him, but we could hear each other. "Hold on a second," I heard myself call out, "I can't move my arm." There was no pain, but my left arm, flung out behind me, was immobile. "Don't move," he called back, "I'll be right over." The second rope team had now caught up to him, and they belayed him across the treacherous moss. We were officially off the climb, but I didn't feel like celebrating the completion of my first wall! By now the adrenaline had worn off and I was suffering wave after wave of relentless pain in my arm and shoulder. Never in my life had I felt such pain, and there was nothing I could do to make it diminish. As the second rope team made their way across, I sat on the ledge and quietly sang over and over a praise song I had learned, having just become a Christian earlier that year:

> *Father, I adore you,*
> *I lay my life before you,*
> *How I love you.*
>
> *Jesus, I adore you…*

Vaguely I heard my friends discussing our options. A helicopter was out. By the time someone could hike out it would be too late in the day, and there was no place on top of the cliff for one to land anyway. We decided the only option was to try to hike out.

Although the ledge on which I landed put us past the technical part of the climb, the path out was still fairly steep and would require some scrambling. My friends put my left arm in a sling and kept my climbing harness on so that one of them could hold onto me from the back. We tried to make it up one way, but it was a no-go: too steep. We started back down in order to try another path. My climbing partner was behind me, holding my harness, when all of a sudden his feet slipped on the steep dirt and he slid down, knocking my feet out from under me. I fell too, landing on my rear. "Oh, my God," he cried, "What have I done?" But my agony had instantly been cut in half! "No, it's okay," I said, "I think my arm is better." My shoulder had been dislocated, and miraculously, the second fall allowed the shoulder to pop back into place! My friend, who was not a Christian but had listened to me sing, "I lay my life before you," looked at me and said, "Maybe there is something to all this God stuff."

We didn't make it back down that night before darkness fell. The guys generously gave me the two climbing ropes to sleep on. Without sleeping bags it was a cold night, and the shivering caused my shoulder to ache, but before long the first hint of light in the east let me know a new day was dawning. I was alive! The day before I had entered the realm of the birds and fallen through thin air, but I was still alive!

As we reached the valley floor, shafts of sunlight pierced the sky directly over Royal Arches. God's masterpiece was once again coming to life. My left arm was so painful I could hardly move it, but with my right I got the camera out of my backpack, and pointing it at God's handiwork, I took the picture you see here. I think that God was smiling with me as the shutter clicked.

Mountains – Day Three of Creation

God called the dry ground "land."
…And there was evening, and there was morning – the third day.   Genesis 1:9-13

On the third day of creation, God gathered the waters into one place and told the dry ground to appear. The result was not just a monotonous expanse of dry ground – a flat plain composed uniformly of dirt. No, just as the rest of God's work bears the stamp of his creativity, the land that appeared was wonderfully diverse: hills and valleys, cliffs and chasms, caves and canyons, and towering over all of these, the mountains.

To my thinking, God took extra care and delight in forming the mountains. The Scriptures say that God himself inhabits a holy mountain. And many of the most significant events in the history of the human race have occurred on top of mountains. When God met with Abraham and stopped him from taking the life of his son Isaac, it was on top of Mt. Moriah. When he appeared face to face with Moses to give him the Law, it was on top of Mt. Sinai. When he came to gather Aaron and Moses at the end of their lives, it was on top of Mt. Hor and Mt. Nebo. When he came to Elijah and showed himself more powerful than the prophets of Baal, it was on top of Mt. Carmel. When he sat between the wings of the cherubim in the holy of holies and met with the high priests, it was on Mt. Zion. When he spoke to Peter, James and John who had just seen Jesus meeting with Moses and Elijah, it was on the Mount of Transfiguration. When he came to strengthen his Son the night before he was crucified, it was on the Mount of Olives. Although God has met with his people in many other places – in deserts, along the shores of lakes, in cities – moun-

tains have played a significant role in the overall story.

God created mountains as wild places, where jagged outcroppings of rock and ice jut forth to pierce the sky. They are home to thin, frigid air and gale force winds. They soar over lake and forest, stream and meadow. Their summits are the first to greet the morning, and the last to let go of evening. They lead a lonely existence – universally admired from a distance, but befriended only by those few with a certain gleam in their eye and a spring in their step.

George Mallory, an English mountaineer who participated in the first three attempts to scale Mt. Everest, was asked by a city-slicker journalist in New York why he would risk life and limb just to climb a mountain. "Because it is there," came the now classic reply. The journal-

> Many of the most significant events in the history of the human race have occurred on top of mountains

ist didn't understand the answer, and Mallory didn't understand how anyone could even ask the question. And so it is for those who have caught "the mountain malady." The heights call to them irresistibly, over and over, higher and higher.

Though attaining the summit of a mountain is a noble and fulfilling pursuit, many are content to just be *in* the mountains. The tools of their craft are not as technical as the climber's; a pair of hiking boots, a backpack, a sleeping bag, and they are ready to venture forth into the wilderness. In America we are blessed to have an extensively developed system of National Parks, as well as State and National Forests. Hundreds of thousands of miles of hiking trails meander through these areas, ensuring that future generations will also be able to explore the wilderness.

The earth is home to many mountain ranges, both large and small. In comparison to the size of the earth, though, even the largest mountain ranges are insignificant bumps. If the earth were the size of a billiard ball, the largest mountains would be less than the size of a speck of dust on the smooth surface. But from our own perspective here on earth, mountains appear anything but small! The largest ranges occur where continental plates collide. Since these plates have roughly the same mass, one plate is not subducted beneath the other, but instead they push against each other and crumple each other up, moving material higher and higher. The Himalayas are the highest mountain range on earth, and also the fastest growing, as the Indian subcontinent continues to push into Eurasia. Large mountain ranges in America include the Sierra Nevada and the Cascades in the West, the Rocky Mountains in the mid-West, and the Appalachians in the East. In addition to the large ranges, there are many other smaller ranges that provide us with mountainous areas. Though few of us actually live in the mountains, most of us don't have to drive too far to get to them.

Why mountains hold such appeal is perhaps best summarized by the title of a classic book on mountaineering: *The Freedom of the Hills*. When we roam the mountains we experience freedom from the typical worries that permeate our existence below. We are able to leave behind the proverbial rat race and revel in what the Creator has made. Henry David Thoreau wrote that "the mass of men lead lives of quiet desperation." In the wilderness we are able to escape such desperation and live in simplicity. John Muir spoke poetically on this theme as well:

> *Climb the mountains and get their good tidings.*
> *Nature's peace will flow into you*
> *as sunshine flows into trees.*
> *The winds will blow their own freshness into you,*
> *and the storms their energy,*
> *while cares will drop off like autumn leaves."*

Mountains are so captivating, and engender such strong feelings of peace and tranquility, that many have been lured into worshipping nature rather than the One who created it. But creators always transcend their creations. We may praise a creation's beauty and intricacy, but worship is to be reserved for the One who wrought such beauty.

I'm delighted to know that our acquaintance with mountains is not just for this life only. When the apostle John was shown a revelation of what would take place in the future, the Spirit of God carried him away "to a mountain great and high," and from that vantage point he saw the New Jerusalem coming down out of heaven from God (Revelation 21:10). The prophet Isaiah is also seeing into the future when he writes, "Come, let us go up to the mountain of the Lord … so that we may walk in his paths" (Isaiah 2:3). Now, that is a mountain I look forward to climbing!

"He who forms the mountains, creates the wind, and reveals his thoughts to man...
the Lord God Almighty is his name."   *(Amos 4:13)*

"Doubly happy, however, is the man to whom lofty mountain-tops are within reach." *John Muir*

"Before the mountains were born or you brought forth the earth and the world,
from everlasting to everlasting you are God."   *(Psalm 90:2)*

"Wilderness is a necessity; mountain parks are useful not only as fountains
of timber and irrigating rivers, but as fountains of life!" *John Muir*

"The sun does not shine for a few trees and flowers, but for the wide world's joy."   *Henry Ward Beecher*

"Shout for joy, O heavens; rejoice, O earth; burst into song, O mountains! For the Lord comforts his people." *(Isaiah 49:13)*

"Do not go where the path may lead, go instead where there is no path."   *Ralph Waldo Emerson*

"Made weak by time and fate, but strong in will to strive, to seek, to find, and not to yield."   *Lord Alfred Tennyson*

"I cling with feeble fingers to the ledge of your great grace." *John Piper*

"Gratitude is the most exquisite form of courtesy."   *Jacques Maritain*

"Everybody needs beauty as well as bread, places to play in and pray in
where nature may heal and cheer and give strength to the body and soul."   *John Muir*

"Live each day as you would climb a mountain. An occasional glance towards the summit puts the goal in mind. Many beautiful scenes can be observed from each new vantage point. Climb steadily, slowly, enjoy each passing moment; and the view from the summit will serve as a fitting climax to the journey." *Joe Porcino*

"On this proud and beautiful mountain we have lived hours of fraternal, warm and exalting nobility.
Here for a few days we have ceased to be slaves and have really been men."   *Lionel Terray*

Interaction with the Creator – An Alpine Adventure

Only once have I had the opportunity to climb a 6,000 meter peak. Huayana Potosi stands at 19,996 feet in the Bolivian Andes. What I remember most of that 18th day of November, 1983, is not so much the last few steps to the summit pyramid, but what took place on the knife edge ridge just a hundred feet below the top.

My journey to the summit really began months earlier when I saw a photo of the Andes and decided that even though I was going to the Amazon jungle to do missionary work, I'd better bring along my ice

axe, crampons and mountaineering boots. My time in the rainforest was fantastic, confirming the call I had felt toward missions after having read the book *Shadow of the Almighty* by Elizabeth Elliott. Like her husband

Jim, who was speared by the Auca Indians, we, too, were on a jungle river, trying to contact a new, unreached nomadic tribe: the Yuqui. After discovering their footprints on a nearby path, we ventured into the jungle to hang bananas, machetes and other gifts to try to convey to them our good intentions. We later learned they were watching us from the other side of the river, spears at the ready. After I left the country, one of the missionaries I accompanied was speared through the chest, but lived and was later able to share his faith with the tribe.

With the call of God on my life to share the good news with those who had never heard, I knew I needed to return to the States to attend Bible college so that I could then join a mission agency. However, there was first the matter of that picture I had seen of the snow-covered Andes. I flew from the rainforest, which is basically at sea level, to the airport in

La Paz, Bolivia, which at 13,313 feet is one of the highest airports in the world. My crampons had acquired a bit of rust after six months in the steaming, humid jungle, so I got out a file and went to work on them until they were gleaming and razor sharp. Not having a friend to accompany me up the mountain, I went in search of a guide and found Bernardo, who had climbed the mountain numerous times. After a couple days of acclimatizing, Bernardo and I set off on our adventure. We spent the first night at 18,700 feet, leaving the tent the following morning about 2 a.m. for our summit bid. Everything went smoothly. The last stretch was steep, but the ice was solid enough and we belayed each other as we moved higher and higher. I was 22, full of youth, strength and the *joie de vivre*. Bernardo took the lead and I belayed him as he made his way to the summit ridge, just one rope length below the top. Then I climbed up to meet him. About 15 feet before I reached him, I stopped and we exchanged a few words in Spanish. He was on a huge block of ice, about the size of a large bedroom. The side of the block was vertical and I'd have to front point a few steps with my crampons to get on top. I swung my ice axe for a purchase, but it bounced off. I swung it again a bit harder. Suddenly, where an instant before there had been Bernardo and the block of ice, now there was nothing. Just silence, and a birds-eye view several thousand feet straight down to the glacier far below. Without pausing to think, I threw myself down the opposite side of the ridge in an attempt to counterbalance Bernardo's fall. An instant later,

there was a terrific jerk on the rope, and then once again all was silent. I started pulling in rope hand over hand – 25 feet, 50 feet, 75 feet – nothing but slack. "Oh, my God," I thought, "the rope broke or was cut in two by the falling ice, and Bernardo is no more." It didn't occur to me until later that if I had been one or two steps farther when the ice block had calved off, I would have shared Bernardo's fate. As I continued to haul in rope, all of a sudden, to my tremendous relief, there was tension on the rope. Something was there! Climbing back up to the ridge I found a shaken Bernardo still in one piece, still attached to the rope. I found out that when the block fell, Bernardo turned in mid air and swung his axe, somehow gaining purchase in the almost vertical west face. The tremendous jerk I felt came as a projection of falling ice caught the rope. Somehow Bernardo had managed to resist the jerk, and then climb back up to the ridge once his wits had returned.

In hindsight we could see that what we thought was the ridge had, in fact, been a huge cornice of overhanging ice. Staying well back from the edge, we ascended the final few steps to the top. Standing on the summit at 19,996 feet, my feet had no way to climb four feet higher, but my lungs thrilled at the chance to suck in that rarified 20,000 foot air. Looking at the surrounding Andes and then down at the glacier far below, we had more than the usual reasons to rejoice. We were alive, surrounded by beauty, and convinced that God was, in fact, not distant in the least!

Oceans – Day Three of Creation

God called the gathered waters "seas." …And there was evening, and there was morning – the third day.   Genesis 1:9-13

On the third day of creation, God not only caused dry ground to appear, but he also gathered all the water into one place. The Scriptures say, "He gave the sea its boundary so the waters would not overstep his command" (Proverbs 8:29). And so the oceans were confined to just over two-thirds of the planet's surface. Most of this vast stretch is barren and monotonously uniform. With an average temperature of 39 degrees Fahrenheit, the sea is generally frigid and uninviting. Ancient peoples traditionally feared the sea, and even the Jews of the Old Testament considered "the deep" to be a place of judgment. Those who ventured forth were often at the mercy of the elements, their feet separated from the solid land of the ocean floor by thousands of feet of water, a world in which large, carnivorous beasts swam. Some feared that if they ventured too far, they would reach earth's end and fall over an imagined edge. God created man with the ability to swim, but the vast distances encountered on the open sea quickly exhaust man's chance of extricating himself if disaster should strike.

But the sea is by no means a barren expanse without purpose. Ninety-seven percent of all the water on earth is saltwater, and the evaporation of this great reservoir provides the means by which freshwater is replenished to the heights. The sea also provides land dwellers with an abundant source of food through an amazing diversity of fish and other sea creatures. And the sea links distant continents, allowing a means of transporting vast quantities of goods from one place to another.

The sea also provides us with the opportunity for adventure and riches. In biblical times, man was faced with the challenge of exploring the sea and returning with exotic items from foreign lands. King Solomon's ships would return to Israel every three years carrying such items as gold and silver, ivory, apes and peacocks. King Ferdinand of Spain commissioned Columbus to sail in search of gold in the West Indies, and thus was discovered the North American continent. Even today, riches under the sands of the Mideast are eagerly sought by huge tankers which cross the sea, each carrying more than a quarter million tons of oil.

The interaction of various forces on the sea means that it is ever changing. A smooth, glassy surface on a calm day is replaced by frothing whitecaps as the wind picks up. Cold masses of air interact with warm oceans, producing hurricanes of tremendous

Waves crash repeatedly against rock, sculpting them into works of art

force. The land under the ocean can also affect the sea's behavior. An earthquake on the sea floor can set off a fast-moving wave, a tsunami, capable of crossing thousands of miles of open water before crashing onto a distant shore. Even the moon, 239,000 miles away, interacts with the ocean, its gravity pulling at the water as it revolves around the earth, causing the ebb and flow of the daily tide.

The occasional monotony of the deep is punctuated by playgrounds of exceptional beauty where water and land meet. Travel posters highlight exotic coves with turquoise water and white sandy beaches. Surfers and waders frolic in 80-degree water while lovers stroll down the beach, stopping occasionally to pick up a cowry shell or a sand dollar. Waves crash repeatedly against rock, sculpting them into works of art, while children sit in the nearby sand and sculpt moats around sand castles.

The coast provides us with some of the most amazing scenery on earth. It is like a magnet, repeatedly drawing us back and appealing to all five of our senses: the noise of the surf, the smell of the salty spray, the taste of seafood, the feel of the refreshing waves and the warm sand. And for our eyes, view after picturesque view with every turn of coastline. With tens of thousands of islands in the world, God has given us more than 500,000 miles of coastline to explore. Most of it is rocky, with bluffs and capes sweeping down to meet the crashing waves. But then there are those gentle meeting places, covered with sand, where the water kisses the land as it gently moves back and forth. We are drawn to such places of beauty where sky and land and water meet. There we can let go the cares of the world. There we are soothed by the murmur of the surf. There we bask in the warmth of the sun. There we experience the raw grandeur of wilderness. Indeed, the coast is where we come face to face with yet another of our Creator's masterpieces.

"In my mind's eye, I visualize how a particular… sight and feeling will appear on a print.
If it excites me, there is a good chance it will make a good photograph.
It is an intuitive sense, an ability that comes from a lot of practice."   *Ansel Adams*

"The world is but a canvas to the imagination."   *Henry David Thoreau*

"Sometimes I get to places just when God's ready to have somebody click the shutter."   *Ansel Adams*

"What we get from this adventure is just sheer joy."   *George Leigh Mallory*

"There is pleasure in the pathless woods … there is rapture on the lonely shore."   *Unknown*

"O Lord, our Lord, how majestic is your name in all the earth! You have set your glory above the heavens." *(Psalm 8:1)*

"In every out thrust headland, in every curving beach, in every grain of sand there is a story…" *Rachel Carson*

"Nature is the art of God."   *Ralph Waldo Emerson*

"Live in the sunshine, swim the sea, drink the wild air…"   *Ralph Waldo Emerson*

"To see a world in a grain of sand, and a heaven in a wild flower,
hold infinity in the palm of your hand, and eternity in an hour."   *William Blake*

"In every walk with nature one receives far more than he seeks." *John Muir*

Interaction with the Creator – Living at the Beach

The beach has always held a special place in my heart. Growing up in the San Francisco Bay Area, our summer treat was heading over the hill to Pajaro Dunes or to the Beach Boardwalk in Santa Cruz. Later in life I had the opportunity to live on the coast for a number of years, first in Senegal, where the beach lay a 15-minute walk over the dunes, and then in Vanuatu in the South Pacific, where we lived just 100 yards from a beautiful black-sand beach. In Senegal we enjoyed boogie boarding and playing in the surf. In Vanuatu we snorkeled above pristine reefs, toyed with clown fish, and followed surreptitiously after sea turtles and manta rays.

While in Vanuatu, as soon as I would get home from work, I would kayak over to Hideaway Island and then snorkel around the exquisite reef which is an underwater marine preserve. I would tie the kayak's rope to my foot while I swam so that it would follow along behind me,

providing a sense of security for when I saw the occasional reef shark and wanted a quick way to exit the water! Once I was snorkeling with my kids at a reef on Epi Island when I saw a BIG shark. Grabbing my seven-year old son, I started towing him toward shore as fast as my flippers would take me, calling after my nine-year old daughter to come along as fast as she could (but not telling her what I had seen). I warned the natives on the beach about the shark but they seemed particularly unimpressed. "We see big ones around here all the time," they told me. I wish I had known that a half hour earlier!

The beach is a wonderful place for photography. The calm glassy sea of today is transformed tomorrow into a turbulent behemoth. Sunny skies alternate with storm clouds to create an ever-changing panoply of light. The sand is washed clean with each high tide, and driftwood is rearranged into new patterns like the turning of a kaleidoscope.

My interest in photography owes more to the beach than my trips there in early years might warrant. As part of an assignment for my first photography class in high school, I started working on a beach scene where we were to combine two images into a single print. I had taken a picture of my five-year old brother playing in the surf, silhouetted by the late afternoon sun. The other image was a close-up of a footprint in the sand. In the darkroom I was attempting to combine the two images. Placing a black and white negative in the Beseler Enlarger, I would first expose the beach scene, dodging a circular area on the beach where I wanted the footprint to go. Then exchanging negatives and adjusting the height and focus on the enlarger, I would expose the second negative on that area of the beach, trying to create a huge footprint in the sand. The title of the photo was to be "Innocence," a statement about the untroubled innocence of youth in a world filled with giants, or at least giant problems.

However, try as I might, every time I put the exposed paper into the developer, what appeared was an obviously contrived photo marked by a circle of light and dark in the area surrounding the footprint. After numerous attempts, my photography teacher suggested that instead of trying to burn the footprint into the middle of the beach, I divide the photo in two and expose the top half first with my brother playing in the surf, and then at the line where the water met the sand, expose the close-up of the footprint so that it would form the whole beach area. As I sloshed the developer back and forth over the next piece of exposed paper and the image started to appear, it was as if magic filled the darkroom. It was perfect! That photo went on not only to win a "Best of Show" in the youth division of a Bay Area photo contest, it also helped me get a job in the darkroom of a local photography shop.

These days, since I'm no longer in a photography class, it is very seldom that I manipulate a photo to such an extent. But I still enjoy photographing the beach in all sorts of conditions. That once got me into trouble when I was taking pictures in the South Pacific of the pounding surf after a hurricane. The waves would occasionally come up over the berm, but when they did I would duck behind a large tree that kept both me and my camera dry. That is, I was dry until one huge wave hit high up on the tree trunk and cast a sheet of water over us both. I quickly ran for a dry towel, but it wasn't too many months later that the electronic connections began corroding and I started getting error messages. Soon it was time to leave an old friend behind. Such days are inevitably sad, reminiscing on all the wonderful places we'd explored together. But then there's that new model with improved features just waiting to be picked up and loved, eager to prove that she, too, can find that special scene.

While living just a few yards from a beach in Vanuatu, we found

that living so close to beauty can carry a price tag. One morning at 4:30 we were literally shaken out of bed by a 7.3 earthquake. We congregated with other neighbors on the front lawn, all of us in our underwear, discussing if there could be a tsunami and if we should flee to higher ground. No tsunami came, but not too many months later we experienced an assault of a different kind, one familiar to those who live by the beach. We spent my birthday mopping up water and praying the house would hold together as 80-100 mph hurricane winds relentlessly screamed outside for hour after hour.

After surviving several small category 1-2 hurricanes, we started to feel a bit more confident. But then we got news of a large category 5 hurricane headed straight for us. Zoe was supposed to hit our island in 24 hours, packing sustained winds of 196 mph with gusts to 236 mph, and a storm surge of 39 feet. Zoe was already on the record books as the most intense tropical cyclone ever observed in the Southern Hemi-

sphere. Being on a small island in the middle of the ocean, there was no way to pack up and drive somewhere out of the storm's path. We urgently sent an E-mail to friends and family back home, apprising them of the hurricane and asking for prayer. As the first rain and wind started to hit our island, the hurricane did a sudden 120° change of direction and headed out again into the open sea. We breathed many sighs of relief intermingled with praise to the One who caused the killer hurricane to divert its path.

Over the years the coast has been a reliable friend. Time and again, the rhythmic crash of the waves calls me back to stroll the beach and play in the surf. And each time I return I see new evidence of the Creator's handiwork as the waters ebb and flow back and forth over his canvas.

Streams and Lakes – Day Three of Creation

In the biblical account, God didn't specifically command streams and lakes to appear, but they are a direct result of his separating the sea from the dry land. As mountains and hills rose out of the sea on that third day, water ran down their flanks. Pulled by gravity, the water droplets started their downward journey, gathering together to form rivulets and brooks, streams and rivers, in an ever increasing crescendo as they made their way back to their source. Divine variations in topography halted the flow in certain locations, and the water accumulated in ponds or lakes, sitting quietly for a time before spilling over the outlet and resuming its downward cascade. Rain later replenished the supply and kept the cycle going. Even though God didn't speak directly of streams and lakes, it was by his design that they exist, and they are like jewels in an already beautiful crown.

In her book *Hinds' Feet on High Places*, Hannah Hurnard describes the song and laughter of water as it answers the call to journey to the lowest place of all. Those who have sat by a babbling brook can identify with that song: "thousands of variations of little trills and murmurs and bubbles and splashing sighs." The song changes as the brook joins together with friends. Now the song is deep and throaty as the water, ever joyful, roars down canyons and over waterfalls. Listening to the water's song is one of the joys of the wilderness. It is a song which changes with each bend in the canyon, with each change of season.

> It is almost as if water is alive, joining with the rest of creation to praise its Maker

Streams call us to their banks for a variety of pursuits. The fisherman stalks the shore, looking for the perfect eddy to cast his fly. The young boy skips stones with his grandpa across a quiet pool. The hiker comes to pump water and slake his thirst after hours on the hot trail. Those who are adventurous raft and kayak through the churning rapids. The engineer seeks a narrow gorge where he can harness the water's force and make electricity. The family comes to picnic and swim. The photographer climbs to a waterfall, where he slows down time to create a silky cascade. Young or old, rich or poor, the stream beckons all of us to come.

It must please the Creator that we enjoy that which he also enjoys. God made streams because he too enjoys them. The apostle John was shown the new heaven and the new earth, and there from under the throne of God and the Lamb flows a river as clear as crystal, containing the water of life. God rejoices as he hears the joyful song of the water. It is almost as if, in some mysterious way, the water is alive, joining with the rest of creation to praise him.

Although there are quiet pools here and there in the rushing streams, God decided to create some larger expanses where the water could rest for a time, and in its stillness reflect other aspects of his creation. When the sky is cloudless and the wind is calm, we see trees and mountains reflected in a deep blue water. Toward sunset, the reflection may turn a fiery gold as the lake takes on the hues of the clouds or the alpenglow on the peaks above. Slight breezes cause the reflection to ripple and dance. Lake water is resting before continuing its downward journey, but it still has a song to sing!

Lakes come in all shapes and sizes, and can be shallow or deep. Hikers swim across small mountain lakes on a warm summer day, but few would consider a 160 mile swim across Lake Superior, the largest lake in America. Some lakes are shallow enough you can wade out almost to the middle. Crater Lake, on the other hand, is 1,932 feet deep. It is the deepest lake in America, and is found in the crater of an extinct volcano. The lake has neither outlet nor inlet, and yet the water level remains constant, with rain and snow exactly replenishing that which is lost to evaporation.

The story of water is really the story of man and of life. We could not live apart from a source of fresh water. In the Old Testament, God presented himself as the one who is "the spring of living water" (Jeremiah 2:13). In the New Testament, Jesus talks to a thirsty woman at a well and tells her that he can give her "living water." He then stands up in a crowd in Jerusalem on the last and greatest day of the Feast of Tabernacles, and calls out, "If anyone is thirsty, let him come to me and drink. Whoever believes in me … streams of living water will flow from within him." (John 7:37-38). The joyful song of the babbling brook is a picture of what happens inside us when faith allows for the release of living water. And oh, what a joyful song the living water makes!

"When words become unclear, I shall focus with photographs.
When images become inadequate, I shall be content with silence."   *Ansel Adams*

"Two roads diverged in a wood, and I – I took the one less traveled by, and that has made all the difference."
Robert Frost

"Discovering this idyllic place, we find ourselves filled with a yearning to linger here,
where time stands still and beauty overwhelms." *Unknown*

"Photography takes an instant out of time, altering life by holding it still."   *Dorothea Lange*

"Never lose an opportunity to see anything that is beautiful.
It is God's handwriting – a wayside sacrament." *Ralph Waldo Emerson*

"Nothing is more beautiful than the loveliness of the woods before sunrise."   *George Washington Carver*

"The Lord your God is bringing you into a good land of flowing streams and pools of water,
with springs that gush forth in the valleys and hills."   *(Deuteronomy 8:7, NLT)*

"Rest is not idleness, and to lie sometimes on the grass under trees on a summer's day, listening to the murmur of the water, or watching the clouds float across the sky is by no means a waste of time."   *J. Lubbuck*

"Like water, be gentle and strong. Be gentle enough to follow the natural paths of the earth, and strong enough to rise up and reshape the world." *Brenda Peterson*

"None know how often the hand of God is seen in a wilderness but them that rove it." *Thomas Cole*

"To the Lord your God belong the heavens, even the highest heavens, the earth and everything in it." *(Deuteronomy 10:14)*

Interaction with the Creator – River Ramblings

It seems I've always associated the smooth, placid water of lakes with relaxation and recreation, while the rushing water of a river speaks to me of adventure. Rivers provide a multitude of challenges. The first challenge is just getting across when your hiking trail continues on the other side. Sometimes it is a simple matter of finding a broad place where the water is not too deep or swift and then just wading across. Other times it can be a bit more technical. I once swam across a raging torrent while trailing a climbing rope, and then set up a Tyrolean traverse across a nar-

row gorge so that the others could follow, suspended high and dry over the crashing water below. Usually when the spring melt caused the streams in the Sierras to swell, it was a matter of putting on tennis shoes, finding a stout stick to serve as a third leg, loosening the belly band on the back-

pack, and slowly making my way across as I faced upstream, trying not to look too much at my next step lest the water spinning by make me dizzy.

On one occasion I was helping guide a group, and we had to cross the Big Arroyo river in Kings Canyon National Park. I went across first, shed my pack on the far bank and then went back into the flow to help the others in case any of them slipped. A girl named Janet did just that. As she was carried downstream, everyone on the bank yelled at her to get out of her backpack. I dove in and swam to her, reaching her just as she was coming out of her pack. Somehow God allowed me to get my feet down and gain a purchase that momentarily stopped us. I grabbed her pack and together we made it to the bank – the adrenaline pumping as we shivered from cold and fright. Then it was back out into the river to make sure the others got safely across.

The other challenge rivers present is how to successfully navigate them. I've done some kayaking and have run some class 5 rapids in a whitewater raft, but my most memorable experience navigating a river happened not in the mountains, but on the flatlands near Chico, California. I was in college and we had a few days off before finals, so my housemate Tim and I decided on a lark to build a raft out of inner tubes and plywood and float down the Sacramento River for a couple days. The river was essentially flat as it made its way through the farmland, and we just soaked in the sun and enjoyed the herons and beaver and other wildlife. The river was at flood stage from the spring rains and we seemed to be moving along at a good clip, but we had no idea how far we had gone because we couldn't see out beyond the levees. So late in the afternoon we stopped at a bridge, climbed up to the road and figured out where we were on our map. To our disappointment we weren't as far as we had hoped, since we had arranged for Tim's mom to pick us up the following day down at Discovery Park. So we decided that instead of tying up our makeshift craft for the night, we'd just keep floating and sleep on board.

All went well until perhaps 11 p.m. when a distant sound woke me up. It was constant and getting louder! Tim and I couldn't see anything, but we started paddling for the shore for all we were worth. However, our cumbersome craft was slow to maneuver, and as we rounded the next bend the glinting moonlight revealed a long line of whitewater rushing over a bypass that was diverting the floodwater down another channel. We fought against the current but were inexorably drawn toward the line of water. As it became apparent that our best efforts to avoid the falls weren't going to succeed, we braced ourselves and over we went! I had visions of my camera disappearing into the river, but amazingly, we made it without capsizing! Our hearts were pounding as we once again dug in and paddled for the bank to tie up for the night. The next morning we took the craft apart, carried the wood and inner tubes back up above the falls to the main river where we reassembled it, and then continued on down the river.

It's not often I get the opportunity to have such a "Tom Sawyer

and Huck Finn experience," but it is precisely those moments that add flavor to life. God probably has a number of angels on call who specialize in protecting us during those times when we add a little salt and pepper to our lives. With God watching over us, we usually emerge from such experiences no worse for wear, but perhaps a bit wiser, and definitely more invigorated!

Flora – Day Three of Creation

Then God said, "Let the land produce vegetation."
…And there was evening, and there was morning – the third day.   Genesis 1:9-13

The theme of variety also characterizes God's creation of flora. Some plants have leaves, others needles. Some have flowers, others fruit. Some prefer sun, others shade. Some are found only in alpine regions, others only in the tropics. What they all have in common is that they produce seed, each according to their kind. Some seeds are eminently familiar – peach pits, pine cones, apple seeds. However for some trees, plants, or grasses, only the most careful observation will reveal how they germinate. Every tender shoot that pushes its head up through the soil should cause us to shake our heads in wonder, amazed at the new birth. As parents we celebrate the advent of our babies. If only we could somehow hear the chorus of the plant kingdom, which crescendos in praise each spring as the earth breaks open to welcome a sea of green.

It is a mystery how vegetation existed on day three since the sun wasn't created until day four, but the light of God's imminent presence was obviously sufficient to sustain his creation. There will be no need of a sun when the new earth is created, and yet vegetation will once again be present and abundant. The third day saw an almost infinite variety of greenery appear: plants and shrubs, trees and bushes, flowers and grasses. The "dry ground" of day two suddenly assumed a majestic air, clothed by a multitude of living organisms, a variety unaccounted for by modern secular science, but wondrously simple to those who have faith in a living and creative God.

Of all the flora, flowers are undoubtedly my favorite (though my taste buds would contend that fruit-bearing trees rate a close second)! Flowers are a delight to the eyes. They paint the landscape in a never ending array of color. Sometimes I sit beside a creek in a mountain meadow and count the species within arm's reach – lupines and columbine, asters and goldenrod, larkspur and monkey flowers. Such flowers are only found in places of beauty – mountain gardens which are perhaps the closest remnant of that first garden where God placed the man and the woman in order to enjoy what he had made.

The sound of the wind blowing through pine needles is another gift from the plant kingdom. Trees are amazing organisms – able to lift water and nutrients hundreds of feet in the air, creators of oxygen through photosynthesis, and suppliers of wood for our fires, our furniture, and a multitude of other objects. The psalmist presents us with an almost fairy-tale image of trees in which they are seen as alive, clapping their hands. And what do they applaud? From the mighty coastal redwood to the stunted whitebark pine, it seems they all are in grateful awe of the Creator's handiwork as he redeems his people and his creation (Isaiah 55:12).

Jesus also acknowledged the beauty of creation. Even a simple flower of the field, he said, is clad finer than the richest and most ornately dressed king in man's history. For the king's clothes are the work of man, but God is the one who made the flower in the field. The hand of man has indeed produced impressive art and magnificent architecture, but the hand of God has far surpassed man's efforts. God is pleased with his handiwork, and desires us to share in admiring what he has accomplished. Is it not the same with us? When we do well on a test, when we try a new recipe, when we publish a book, when we finish a masterpiece, we eagerly seek out a loved one so that they might see what we've accomplished and rejoice with us.

The globalization of the world marketplace means that the produce section at the grocery store is now much more colorful in winter months than in years past. Strawberries and grapes are available year round, and items such as mangoes, which were previously considered exotic, are now becoming commonplace. However our culinary experience only scratches the surface of the tremendous variety God created for man to enjoy. In our family's travels as missionaries, we have lived in a number of places where some fruits and nuts are only found in the immediate area and only have locally known names. My daughter was born in Senegal and grew up in a remote African village. Perhaps the third word she learned was a five syllable word for a local fruit the village kids used to bring to us. As a linguist interested in the process of language development, I would just scratch my head in wonder at my daughter's vocabulary: "Ma-ma," "Da-da" and "kitakaliya"! There were a dozen or so wild fruits that grew out in the bush, all of them different than anything we'd ever tasted before or since, all of them equally impossible to describe to someone who has never seen or tasted them. But they provided my children's fondest memories of growing up – disappearing on the African plains for hours at a time with a band of their friends, discovering exotic varieties that seem to have been hiding since Eden. If only it were possible to tour the whole earth, we would stand amazed at the nameless variety of delicacies God has placed in our hands.

Since it was man who sinned in the Garden of Eden it might seem perhaps unfair that God cursed the *ground*. But the creation was indeed changed, rendering man's livelihood a chore, as well as introducing difficulty and death where none such existed before. The ground now produces thorns and thistles (and poison oak) as it groans, longing for redemption. The story of redemption is marked in the Bible by the bookends of the Tree of Life. In fact the theme of the whole Bible could be "The Story of the Tree of Life." How man once had access to the tree in the beginning of Genesis, how he was driven from it as a result of his sin, and how in the last chapters of Revelation he once again gains access to it through Christ's redemptive work. What a special tree that must be, that God would assign his most powerful angels to guard it. What a privilege it will be to one day partake of the fruit it will yield each month (Rev 22:2). The flora of Eden will once again be available to mankind, but a mankind with open eyes, aware of both evil and good. Those who hunger and thirst for righteousness will take and eat the fruit. They will be given their heart's desire and be made pure. They will no longer be surrounded by evil since God has ensured that the tree of life isn't available where any impurity exists. Just think, no more injustice, no drugs, no abuse, no immorality, no cheating, lying, drunkenness, swearing, no garbage, no crime, no traitors – to sum it up no more *curse*. On that day we'll hear the trees once again clapping their hands. We'll see flowers of indescribable beauty waving in the wind. We'll taste new kinds of fruit that will make our taste buds sing with joy. The present creation is a testimony to God's amazing handiwork, but the new creation will surpass even the original Eden before the fall. Ahh … what a hope we have in Christ!

> God is pleased with his handiwork, and desires us to share in admiring what he has accomplished

"Since the creation of the world God's invisible qualities... have been clearly seen." *(Romans 1:20)*

"The miracles of nature do not seem miracles because they are so common. If no one had ever seen a flower, even a dandelion would be the most startling event in the world."   *Anonymous*

"I believe a leaf of grass is no less than the journey-work of the stars."   *Walt Whitman*

"The greatest wonder is that we can see these trees and not wonder more."   *Ralph Waldo Emerson*

"A true photograph need not be explained, nor can it be contained in words."   *Ansel Adams*

If future generations are to remember us with gratitude rather than contempt, we must leave them more than the miracles of technology. We must leave them a glimpse of the world as it was in the beginning, not just after we got through with it." *President Lyndon B. Johnson (upon signing of the Wilderness Act, 1964)*

"Each season has its own wonder, its own special place and purpose in the pattern of creation."   *Unknown*

"Each moment of the year has its own beauty."   *Ralph Waldo Emerson*

"I went to the woods because I wished to live deliberately, to front only the essential facts of life, and see if I could not learn what it had to teach, and not, when I came to die, discover that I had not lived."   *Henry David Thoreau*

"In the wilderness I find something more dear than in the streets … in the woods we return to reason and faith."
Ralph Waldo Emerson

"Blessed is the man who perseveres under trial, because when he has stood the test, he will receive the crown of life…"
(James 1:12)

"Flowers appear on the earth; the season of singing has come."   *(Song of Songs 2:12)*

"The few little years we spend on earth are only the first scene in a Divine Drama that extends into Eternity."
Edwin Markham

"Happiness lies in the joy of achievement and the thrill of creative effort."   *Franklin D. Roosevelt*

"In the wilderness the sanctity of life is felt – joyfully and with such intensity, as to leave us with a sense of conviction."
Phil Arnot

"The earth laughs in flowers."   *E.E. Cummings*

Interaction with the Creator – The Valley of the Magical Snags

One of my favorite books growing up was *My Side of the Mountain* by Jean George, the story of a young boy who spent a year living off the land in a hollowed-out tree. I was never able to do that, but as a youth I did have a tree that was my refuge – a large pine in our backyard where I would climb to the top, attach my climbing rope and then rappel back down. It was a way to momentarily escape life in the city and keep alive my dream of returning to the mountains as soon as the summer break arrived. Another thing I did to keep my dream alive was to carve the names of the mountains I had climbed in a large piece of redwood I had found on a trail at the coast. That didn't last too long though. After the 28th peak there wasn't room to inscribe any more.

Although I never had the chance to live exclusively off the land, I was interested in all the plants and trees that God had made. We often took flower and tree guides on our trips to the Sierras, and before long I was able to identify most of the common species. The guides mentioned which ones the native Indians had used for food, and I would try them as well. Later, when I lived overseas as a missionary, I found that our neighbors relied heavily on the various plants and trees in the bush to supplement their daily diet. We also learned which ones were tasty, and which ones were

useful for other purpose (such as providing a bit of cover when it started to rain)! When we returned to the States on furlough, our kids loved going to Lake Damariscotta in Maine where Grandma and Grandpa Schluntz leased a cabin every summer. We would canoe over to a small island we dubbed Blueberry Island and gorge ourselves on wild blueberries. Our purple mouths were a testimony that there is something almost magical about eating food right from its source.

One place that held magic for me in my high school years was the headwaters of Laurel Creek in Kings Canyon National Park, just southeast of Mineral King. The bench just above the creek was full of magnificent snags. A friend told me of the place, saying there were hundreds of dead whitebark pines that were gnarled into all sorts of fantastic shapes. With just a bit of imagination you could find dragons and unicorns and all sorts of magical creatures there. I was in awe as I walked through the valley, camera in hand. The swirls and whorls and knots in the old snags transformed them into works of art. Some members of our

group climbed onto the backs of mythical creatures and pretended we were in C.S. Lewis' allegorical world, Narnia, riding into battle with the great lion Aslan. Soon however, we were rudely brought back to the 20th century as two fighter jets streaked over us, just a few hundred feet off the ground. They were evidently on a training exercise, hugging the ground with their terrain-following radar and flying at mach speed so we had no warning of their approach until the noise of their burners knocked us off our mighty wooden steeds. But the magic returned as

quickly as the noise receded, and on we went through the valley of the snags, the forest punctuated only by the sound of laughter as we gleefully spied other creatures frozen in the timeless wood.

In the course of our lives, fantasy and adventure tend to recede with age. To engage in dreams and to strike out for new destinations requires a dedicated effort. For those who don't forget to invest in such pursuits, their lives are immeasurably richer, filled with the memorial stones of many happy memories.

The Heavens – Day Four of Creation

And God said, "Let there be lights in the expanse of the sky."
…And there was evening, and there was morning – the fourth day. Genesis 1:14-19

The Bible is a book which largely focuses on the story of earth and the story of mankind. On the fourth day of creation, we read that God created two bodies in the sky to give light to the earth, the greater to govern the day and the lesser to govern the night. Then, sandwiched in the middle of a description of the purpose of the sun and moon, we read five simple words that almost seem to be an afterthought: "He also made the stars" (Genesis 1:16). Nothing else is said about the stars until God tells Abraham that his descendants would be as numerous as the stars in the sky. "Look up at the heavens and count the stars – if indeed you can count them," God tells Abraham (Genesis 15:5). On a clear, moonless night, without the pollution of the industrial revolution, Abraham might have been able to see as many as 9,600 stars with the naked eye. That is a lot of descendants for a very old man who had remained childless his entire married life. But it is less than a drop in a bucket compared to all the descendants that God planned to give Abraham.

God also uses another image to communicate to Abraham how copious his descendants would be: "Your descendants will be as numerous as the sand on the seashore" (Genesis 22:17). Now there is something Abraham can get his hands on, something that really communicates the vastness of God's promise! Just as it is difficult to count individual stars as they scintillate and move across the sky (did I already count that one over there?), it's also difficult to count individual grains in a handful of sand. But Abraham knew that each handful had thousands of grains, and

he knew he could spend months and years and never even come close to counting how many handfuls were at a single beach.

We have been told there are a lot of stars. Modern telescopes have allowed us to see what prior generations could only imagine. The age of discovery continues, but today we know that there are at least 100 billion stars in our galaxy, the Milky Way. And there are billions of galaxies, each with billions of stars. The numbers are so large they almost become meaningless. Perhaps the best way to think of such large numbers is to run our hands through the sand, as Abraham did. Usually when we think of grains of sand, we think of the beach. But let's imagine that the whole world is a beach, and that the sand covers not only the exterior of the planet, but makes up the interior as well. A sphere of that size would contain approximately 10^{20} grains of sand. Guess what? There are still more stars. Hundreds of times more!

Not only are we amazed at the number of stars, but their size also boggles the mind. There are stars so large that if our solar system were inside one of them, not only would the earth comfortably be able to revolve around the sun, but also the next most distant planets: Mars, Jupiter and Saturn. Now those are huge stars!

Not only is the size of stars amazing, but their variety is as well. There are stars called neutron stars which are so dense that a quantity the size of a dime weighs 100 million tons. And there are stars even denser than that, called black holes, which have gravitational fields so strong that even light isn't able to escape. There are at least nine black holes in our galaxy alone. There are also stars so bright that their core temperatures are in excess of 10 million degrees Celsius. These blue supergiants convert their mass to energy thousands of times faster than our own sun does, and they appear in telescopes as extremely bright objects. They often end their lives in spectacular explosions called supernovas.

Another aspect of space that challenges our ability to comprehend it is its vastness. The distances between the various stars and the various galaxies are staggering. We are forced to use a unit of measurement involving the fastest known object in the universe. Light travels 186,000 miles in a second, or 5.9 trillion miles in a year. But even at that incredible speed, it would take light 120,000 years just to traverse our own galaxy. To arrive at some of the more distant galaxies that have been discovered would take more than 15 billion years.

> Perhaps God made space so immense in order to remind us just how big he really is

Although comprehending the distances involved in space taxes our minds, the Scriptures say that God "marked off the heavens with the breadth of his hand" (Isaiah 40:12). The distances are not vast to him. It is rather he who is vast! To say we serve a big God is an understatement! Perhaps God made space so immense in order to remind us just how big he really is. If ever we doubt whether God is capable of helping us in our difficulties, we have only to lift our eyes and contemplate the heavens.

Whereas the Bible primarily relates the story of man and his sojourn on earth, we catch glimpses of other orders of created beings. The cherubim are different than the seraphim. The twenty-four elders are different than the four living creatures who have six wings and are covered with eyes. And then there are angels and archangels. We know only the briefest of details concerning these other beings. When were they created? Where did they live? Was redemption also somehow part of their story? With so much still to learn, who could ever imagine that heaven might be boring!

The first human ever to venture into space was Yuri Gagarin, a Russian Cosmonaut. As he orbited the earth, he reportedly said, "I don't see any God up here." Evidently he had his eye out for a rather smallish god, a provincial god, a god visible to the human eye. But the Creator of the universe is neither small nor visible. He is spirit, and he is spiritually discerned. And yet he has left his imprint on the physical world he created. From the fine brush work at the subatomic level, to the wide brush marks which paint the galaxies, the universe unequivocally testifies that a master Designer has been at work. "The heavens declare the glory of God" (Psalm 19:1). How can we do anything except join the chorus? Praise be to our God and Creator!

"Just look at the universe – God's fingerprints are all over it."   *Unknown*

"For the scientist who has lived by his faith in the power of reason … he has scaled the mountains of ignorance; he is about to conquer the highest peak; as he pulls himself over the final rock, he is greeted by a band of theologians who have been sitting there for centuries." *Robert Jastrow, astronomer with NASA*

"Your love, O Lord, reaches to the heavens, your faithfulness to the skies."   *(Psalm 36:5)*

"When a man takes one step toward God, God takes more steps toward that man than there are sands in the worlds of time."
The Work of the Chariot

"The universe … appears to me as a text written in invisible ink, of which in our
rare moments of grace we are able to decipher a small segment."   *Arthur Koestler*

"He wraps himself in light as with a garment; he stretches out the heavens like a tent."   *(Psalm 104:2)*

Interaction with the Creator – Watching the Night Sky

Some people these days have the opportunity to buy a seat on a rocket and take a trip into space, but the vast majority of us have to appreciate the heavens from our more modest stance on earth. I once spent a sleepless night at high altitude without gear, watching the stars on their slow journey across the night sky. The heavens were brilliant and the glittering stars were amazing, but I have to admit that most of the time I was searching for the first rays of sunshine to come and warm my shivering frame.

It happened the summer of 1982 when I was working as a mountaineering guide for Sierra Treks. The owner of the outfit had recently gotten engaged, and he wanted his fiancé Katie to experience the wonders of the alpine world. He had lost both hands and feet to frostbite on a climb of McKinley several years earlier, so he asked me if I would take her up the north face of the Matterhorn, located above Bridgeport in Yosemite National Park on the eastern side of the Sierras. The route on the north face is a fairly easy 5.6 climb, but it has a number of pitches and a lot of exposure, which give it somewhat of a big wall feel.

There were three of us on the outing. We hiked in and spent the night at Twin Lakes, and then got off to an early start the following morning, confident we'd be back down by late afternoon. Because the way down would involve descending the East Couloir, we had to carry ice axes, crampons and boots, in addition to our rock climbing gear. We also had food and water, a first aid kit, my camera, and we each threw in a long sleeve shirt and pants even though the summer day promised to be a warm one. So our packs were heavy and on difficult pitches we had to haul them up separately.

Our progress up the mountain went slower than planned. Katie had never climbed before and having one rope team with three people meant I had to belay two people up to me before leading the next pitch. We were just one rope length below the top when our daylight ran out. We put on our long clothes and huddled together on a ledge as the stars came out in full force and the Milky Way began its slow dance across the sky.

Even in the middle of summer it gets pretty cold in the Sierras above 12,000 feet. We talked of sleeping bags and pizza and the Travertine natural hot springs east of Bridgeport where we had luxuriated in hot, steamy water just the week before. None of us got any sleep, but by stomping our feet on our little ledge and huddling together we didn't get frostbite either. With no moon and no clouds the stars glittered like diamonds above us. Impatiently we awaited the arrival of earth's nearest star. After what seemed like an eternity the distant stars started to fade and the eastern sky took on the first hues of pink.

Shortly thereafter I started up the last pitch to the top. It was not particularly difficult except for the fact that my bones and joints were so stiff with cold. Once we had completed it though, we all agreed it would have been foolish to have attempted it in dim light the night before. We stood on the summit and cheered the arrival of the sun, reveling in the first rays to break the horizon, and knowing that warmth would soon follow.

An unexpected bivouac on the side of a cliff is generally not the best way to entice a novice to fall in love with the alpine world, but Katie accepted it with good cheer. In the end it is those epic adventures that remain in our minds and get retold over and over, long after the ordinary excursion has faded into the background.

Since that day I've slept on top of many different mountains, though never again without gear. There is something inherently wild and special about being on a summit at sunset and sunrise. The colors are more vivid, the wind is brisker, and the solitude is poignant. And as you lay in your bag and look up into the night sky, heaven is just an arm's length away.

Fish and Fowl – Day Five of Creation

And God said, "Let the water teem with living creatures, and let birds fly above the earth."
…And there was evening, and there was morning – the fifth day. Genesis 1:20-23

Before making animals to walk upon the earth, God created species that would fly through the sky and breathe underwater. When God commanded that the water teem with living creatures, the Hebrew uses a term which literally means "to swarm." Indeed the sea is filled with life, and not with just a limited number of species, but a vast multitude. Fish come in a veritable rainbow of colors. Some, like the male anglerfish, measure just a quarter of an inch, while other fish like the whale shark are over 60 feet long. There are more than 230 species of minnows in North America alone. Some sea creatures have gills and obtain oxygen from the water while others have lungs and breathe in air from the surface. Not only is there diversity in color and size but in shape as well. Consider how different the octopus is from the lobster and the barracuda from the clown fish.

Just as the waters teem with life, so does the sky. Everywhere on earth we find birds of all different colors, sizes and shapes. Some eat seeds and berries while others are carnivores. Some have short stubby wings adapted to quick flight through branches, while others have broad wingspans which help them to soar on the thermals. Some like the hummingbird have long, thin beaks, allowing them to drink nectar, while others like the woodpecker have short, stout beaks, allowing them to break open nuts or create hiding places in trees to store their find for another day. Hawks and eagles soar high above the earth as they hunt, their keen eyesight picking up the movement of tiny rodents far below.

Flycatchers and orioles pursue their prey up close, performing amazing aerobatic feats as they snatch mosquitoes and other insects out of midair.

Although the variety of species in the animal kingdom staggers the intellect, we still have not yet classified all the various life forms God has created. At times we are confronted with the extinction of certain species as man's influence on the earth increases. The tragedy of their loss is mitigated only by the continual discovery of new species that are classified in our taxonomies almost without our knowledge. Just this week I read an article on the Internet with the title "52 new species found in Indonesian reefs." Not long before that I read about a sighting of an ivory billed woodpecker, a species that was previously thought extinct, since the last documented sighting was in the 1940s.

Not only has our exploration of the planet allowed us to add new species to our taxonomies, but we have even discovered organisms that have caused us to reevaluate our most basic definition of what constitutes a life form. Previously, viruses were not considered to be alive, since they require a host cell in order to survive. But now many biologists consider them to be living parasites, since they contain genetic material and reproduce. If they are indeed living organisms, then the number of life forms available to catalogue has increased dramatically.

> The variety of species in the animal kingdom staggers the intellect

Also in recent times, scientists have been able to journey to places on this earth that were inaccessible to man just a few decades ago. Using special deep-diving research submarines, oceanographers have sampled volcanic vents in the sea floor. These regions are in utter darkness, under extreme heat and pressure, and with incredibly high PH levels, and yet scientists have found life here. And not just one or two species struggling for survival, but a whole classification of organisms called Euryachaeota which thrive in just such an environment. Our understanding of what constitutes life and where we find it continues to develop as we gain the ability to explore new and uncharted regions.

Not only has the exploration of the deep fascinated man, but taking to the heavens has intrigued him as well. In more recent times man has succeeded in transporting himself across the sky and even into space. But to journey underwater or into the air is a complex task requiring the help of sophisticated machinery. We gaze with envy at the hawk who simply spreads his wings, and seemingly without any effort at all, lifts himself into the air.

God has created each animal for a special niche. Only rarely do we find one, such as the duck, who is equally comfortable walking on land, flying through the air, or swimming in water. We humans typically like our feet on solid ground. But that has not hindered us from making short excursions into the air or water. In fact, what we have learned from the birds and fish has allowed us to extend our visits into their worlds.

The Psalmist, contemplating the variety of species God created, concludes the following:

> *How many are your works, O Lord!*
> *In wisdom you made them all;*
> *the earth is full of your creatures.* (Psalm 104:24)

Cecil Frances Alexander, a more modern psalmist, penned a similar sentiment:

> *All things bright and beautiful,*
> *All creatures great and small,*
> *All things wise and wonderful,*
> *The Lord God made them all.*

"I know every bird in the mountains, and the creatures of the field are mine."   *(Psalm 50:11)*

"One cannot be lonesome where everything is wild and beautiful and busy and steeped with God."   *John Muir*

"Every day should be passed as if it were to be our last."   *Publilius Syrus*

"But ask the animals, and they will teach you, or the birds of the air, and they will tell you;
which of all these does not know that the hand of the Lord has done this?"   *(Job 12:7,9)*

"Every bird of the mountains and all the animals of the field belong to me."   *(Psalm 50:11)*

"The best remedy for those who are afraid, lonely or unhappy is to go outside, somewhere where they can be quiet, alone with the heavens, nature and God. Because only then does one feel that all is as it should be and that God wishes to see people happy, amidst the simple beauty of nature."   *Anne Frank*

"When love and skill work together, expect a masterpiece."   *John Ruskin*

"Praise the Lord from the earth, you great sea creatures and all ocean depths."   *(Psalm 148:7)*

"To the eyes of the man of imagination, nature is imagination itself."   *William Blake*

"Nothing great was ever achieved without enthusiasm."   *Ralph Waldo Emerson*

Interaction with the Creator – A Fish Story

I think everyone has at least one "big fish story" – that magical time when the line went taut and whatever was pulling on the other end was bigger than anything you expected. But those experiences are usually preceded by many ordinary days of fishing when the catch is more commonplace. I remember the first time I ever fished as a young boy, with my grandpa showing me how to cast and patiently untangling my snarled line. Fishing became my passion for a couple years, and in the winter I would tie washers to my line and practice casting in the backyard so that when summer arrived I'd be able to drop the lure exactly where I wanted in a mountain brook.

Fishing for trout in the Sierras was what I enjoyed most. There were rainbows, goldens, German browns and brook trout. The backpacking trips I went on were between 10 and 17 days, so having a few extra fish to supplement the food we carried was always welcome. I carried a light telescoping rod and a small open faced reel loaded with six pound monofilament test line. Most of our trips were off trail, so we came to streams and lakes that saw only a few fishermen a year. Early in the summer, the fish would sometimes be so ravenous that I could hook one with my #2 rooster tail on every single cast. Other times they would be so wily that my stringer would be empty no matter what lure or method I tried.

When I think of the most fish I ever took in, it was not by using a special lure, but by a more unconventional method. One summer I worked with my brother-in-law, stocking fish for the Department of Environmental Protection in Connecticut. Part of our job was to sample what fish were in each lake, and so we would go out in a boat after dark and shock the fish using special high-voltage equipment. Twenty or thirty fish around the boat would go belly up, momentarily stunned, and we would scoop them up in nets to measure and weigh them before throwing them back in and then moving on to another location. There were always some big ones, but of course, landing fish like that removes the fun of trying to entice them to bite a hook, and then struggling to reel them in.

When I went to Bolivia in the '80s, I found the Amazon River unlike anything I had ever experienced back in the States. A missionary showed me how the water would boil with piranhas if you threw in some fish guts. As we paddled along at night, twin red beams would often reflect back as our flashlight passed over the eyes of crocodiles that lined the banks of the river. Just getting to the missionary's house proved to be a challenge. When the small mission plane we were in touched down on

the grass airstrip, the landing gear on one side buckled, causing the propeller to hit the ground and forcing us off the runway. We came to a stop with buzzers wailing in the cockpit and the pilot's terse words, "Everybody out NOW!"

One evening after work, we went down to the river, tied some bait to a huge hook, and attaching a size D battery as a sinker, we cast our 100 pound test lines into the river and secured them to a log on shore. We didn't have any fishing poles, but my friend told me that when we returned in the morning, anything we'd caught would be tired enough we could just pull it in by hand. When we arrived at the river's edge the next morning, I was dismayed to find that my line must have got hung up on a snag. I pulled but nothing budged – there was just a steady resistance. But then, oddly, the resistance slightly increased and then slightly lessened. What was going on? Little by little, hand over hand, I managed to take in the line. What finally showed up was a 60 pound sting ray that had

swallowed the bait. Although most of the fight had gone out of him, I found as he approached shore that there was still a little left! Making headway against the river's steady current with something that size and shape was a challenge, and the line cut into my hand as I struggled to land him. Finally I got him ashore – a dark saucer that almost matched the color of the mud on the bank (see adjoining photo). It wasn't what we had set out to catch, but it did give me a good fish story I could write about to the folks back home!

Many years have passed and for me other pursuits have largely replaced the challenge of catching fish. But I still see the magic in the eyes of my kids. As I sit on the banks of the Applegate River on a warm summer day, I'll hear the sound of splashing, and I'll look up from my book to see twinkling eyes and huge grins and one of my kids yelling, "Dad, I think I've got a big one!"

Fauna – Day Six of Creation

And God said, "Let the land produce living creatures."
…And there was evening, and there was morning – the sixth day. Genesis 1:24-31

Just as God created incredible variety in the plant kingdom on the third day of creation, he was also busy on the sixth day as he filled the earth with organisms that aren't rooted to just one spot. Some of his creatures have fur and claws, others have hair and hooves, while others have eight legs and spin webs. Some swing from trees, some slither across the ground, while others burrow into the earth. Some live on the freezing tundra, while others live in steaming jungles. Carnivores and herbivores, vertebrates and invertebrates, cold blooded and warm blooded, nocturnal and diurnal – God has filled the earth with a wonderfully diverse array of creatures.

Before man sinned, he ate from the various trees in the Garden of Eden. At that time, animals were man's companions, never his meal. But like so much else, that changed as a result of man's sin. Death entered Eden on the day Adam and Eve disobeyed God. Their eyes were opened and they now saw they were naked. To hide their shame, God clothed them in garments of skin. Blood was poured out on ground that was never meant to see blood. It was the first sacrifice, a sacrifice that could not atone for sin, but could only hide its shame until a more perfect blood could be offered. And so the first of God's creation lost its life – an animal.

As man's sin increased on the earth, his relationship with the animal kingdom changed. God said, "The fear and dread of you will fall upon all the beasts of the earth … everything that lives and moves will be food for you" (Genesis 9:2-3). Now, rather than man hiding from God, it is animals who hide from man. The rabbit, the fox, the wolf – in the wild we see them rarely, and only for a few seconds before they are running for cover. Normally such sightings cause us to marvel at their beauty and speed. Perhaps instead we should be sorrowful that they are fleeing where once they would have approached for a kind word and a caress.

Although the fear of man is present in a great majority of animals, God also ordained for man to have dominion over them. So man rules over the animal kingdom. Man has been able to tame even the most ferocious species. We see movies with trained grizzly bears or lions featured in the starring role. We go to water parks where killer whales tow trainers from their dorsal fins. And we see cobras rising out of a basket to the sound of a flute, ready to strike their mortal enemy, and yet not daring.

God has not left us completely bereft of friendly companionship with the animal world. He gave us a few domestic species which willingly remain by our side. And so dogs have earned the sobriquet "man's best friend," with cats rating a close second.

> God has filled the earth with a wonderfully diverse array of creatures

One interesting animal that has won the hearts of many is the horse. It exists in both the wild, where it is fearful of man, and in barns, where it is content to do his bidding. For some reason, horses are favored by young teenage girls. My own daughter fell in love with the equine world at age nine. How incongruous to see a magnificent animal, well over a thousand pounds of rippling muscle, being controlled by a sixty pound girl. Just a couple of bucks or kicks and he could be free and back in the wild, but not only does the horse acquiesce to dominionship, he will even lay down his life if asked. This was attested over and over in the days of the wild West, when in an attempt to save their own lives, men had to ask from their horse everything it had to give.

As humans we are fairly well acquainted with the animals that approach the top of the food chain. But the vast majority of animals fan out in a gigantic pyramid to support those at the top. It is said that if one were to weigh all the ants in the world, their weight would surpass that of the combined weight of the entire human race. That's a lot of ants! While larger mammals are easily recognizable, many other species require a microscope even to be seen. It's estimated that to support a blue whale for just one day, a half million krill must give up their lives. Often we are oblivious of the multitudes at the bottom of the chain who give their lives that we might live.

We are also largely ignorant of the many animals that previously lived on the earth but are now extinct. Some, like the dinosaur and the wooly mammoth, lived in the distant past. Others became extinct more recently, like the Tasmanian Tiger, or Thylacine, the last one dying in captivity just 65 years ago. Australian scientists report they are working on a way to revive the Tasmanian Tiger using cloning technology. Others dream of reviving more distant species, transforming Jurassic Park from the realm of fiction to non-fiction.

Although it may be possible in the future to become reacquainted with extinct species, it's also possible that we might have to wait until the new heavens and the new earth are created to see pterodactyls in flight. Some wonder if there really will be animals in heaven. The Scriptures are largely silent on the matter, and yet Paul wrote that the whole creation, which includes animals, is groaning along with man, waiting for redemption, and that it too will be liberated from bondage (Romans 8:20-23). Isaiah tells us that the wolf will one day feed together with the lamb, and the lion will eat straw like an ox (Isaiah 65:25). This will take place on the new earth. There have been several dogs I've loved in this life, and I wouldn't be surprised to see them exuberantly wagging their tails, ready to lick my hand when I make my appearance at the appointed time.

God created one particularly amazing animal which provides us with perhaps the greatest illustration of what it means to be a Christian. The caterpillar starts his humble life crawling in the dirt. But he then goes through a transformation, emerging from a cocoon with beautifully colored wings, and able to soar across the sky. This transformation is analogous to the Greek word, *metamorphoō*, from which we get our present day term, metamorphosis. When Jesus led Peter, James and John to the top of the Mount of Transfiguration, the text says he "metamorphosed" before them (Mark 9:2). In Romans 12:2 Paul tells believers not to conform any longer to the pattern of this present world, but to "metamorphose" our minds. And in 2 Corinthians 3:18 he goes on to say that as we behold the Lord of glory, we are being "metamorphosed" into his likeliness with ever increasing glory. What hope the butterfly gives us! We are being transformed, we are growing wings, we are leaving the dirt of sin behind and we are taking to the sky. We are not becoming angels, but we are becoming who God has always intended us to be!

"We have only this moment, sparkling like a star in our hand and melting like a snowflake. Let us use it before it is too late." *Marie Beyon Ray*

"All good things are wild and free."   *Henry David Thoreau*

"Friends have all things in common."   *Plato*

"The heavens are yours, and yours also the earth; you founded the world and all that is in it." *(Psalm 89:11)*

"Animals are such agreeable friends – they ask no questions, they pass no criticisms."   *George Eliot*

"Happiness is as a butterfly which, when pursued, is always beyond our grasp,
but which if you will sit down quietly, may alight upon you."   *Nathaniel Hawthorne*

"In his hand is the life of every creature and the breath of all mankind."   *(Job 12:10)*

"Let every creature praise his holy name for ever and ever."   *(Psalm 145:21)*

"In all things of nature there is something of the marvelous."   *Aristotle*

"With my great power and outstretched arm I made the earth and its people and the animals that are on it."
(Jeremiah 27:5)

Interaction with the Creator – Approaching Wildlife

I went on my first solo backpacking trip when I was 17 years old. It was an eleven day trip, and I planned to be off trail for as much of the time as possible. My route was through some of the most wild and remote country in Kings Canyon National Park. This was long before the days of cell phones, and I knew that if something went wrong, no one would even begin to start looking for me until the eleven days were up. I felt confident in my backcountry skills, but there was always the unforeseen, the unexpected. What frightened me most were rattlesnakes. I planned to climb up through the Enchanted Gorge to the Ionian Basin, and I had heard it was chock full of rattlers. But I really wanted to go there after seeing an incredible photo of a peek called the Charybdis reflected in a lake at the top of the gorge in Phil Arnot's book, *The Mystique of the Wilderness*.

I got to the Enchanted Gorge on the sixth day of my trip, and picking up a stout stick, I started to make my way up the steep canyon over very rough terrain. Every thirty seconds or so I would shout out "snake" and then tap the rocks around me with the stick, hoping that either my voice or the vibrations would warn any snake in my path that I was passing through. It seemed to work. After a few hours, I had not heard the whirr of a single set of rattles (nor seen any other wildlife, but that was okay with me just as long as I didn't meet up with any snakes)! The climb was difficult with a full pack and it was very hot, so after a couple hours I stopped by the creek and sat in the shade of a snow bank to rest and get a drink. I had been there perhaps ten minutes when three feet from me a rattlesnake popped his head over a rock. Since I hadn't been making any noise, he didn't know I was there! We both saw each other at the same moment – he gave one serious shake of his rattles and then, to my relief, took off the other way.

The encounter with the snake gave fresh encouragement to my litany of calling out and striking rocks with my stick as I continued up the gorge. I reached the 8,500 foot level with no further mishap and breathed a sigh of relief, knowing I was now above the altitude where most rattlesnakes are found. Now that I was once again a silent participant in the natural surroundings, I was much more likely to see other creatures God had created. I didn't have long to wait. After I reached the lake that afternoon I had an encounter with a more friendly species. Following is an excerpt from my journal:

"I just spent 45 minutes photographing two marmots. They were initially about twenty feet away and growling at each other because they were both trying to eat from the same clump of grass. I got my camera out of my pack and slowly walked toward them, but they got scared and

ran away. About seven minutes later they were back again, and this time I slithered over on my stomach. I must have taken five or six pictures and eventually got to within three feet of them. Every little while I would try to imitate their whistle so that they would look at me or stand up on their hind legs and then I'd take the photo. I kept on having to open up my aperture because the sun was going down. I took all the marmot shots at 1/125th second from F5.6 to F2.8. After a while they moved off and wouldn't come back. I guess they figured I was encroaching on their food, so one of them decided to reciprocate. He went over, climbed up on my backpack, and started looking for a way inside. When I turned around to try and get a picture he took off again. Anyway, I've decided that I'll now leave him and his food alone if he does likewise with mine."

In the early days when all I had was a 50mm prime lens, it was a rare occasion indeed when I could get a close-up of a wild animal. Today I have a long zoom lens, and although the pursuit is somewhat easier, there is still that same sense of euphoria when one of God's wild creatures fills the frame of my viewfinder.

The Psalmist said that God made his feet to be like those of a deer, enabling him to stand on the heights (Psalm 18:33). What a day it will be when we all have feet like hind's feet and are able to skip to and fro with ease across the mountain heights. Until that day, I'll continue to lace up my hiking boots. I may not be able to keep up with my four-legged friends, but I sure enjoy watching them as they race across God's canvas!

I spent the last night of my solo backpack at 13,568 feet on top of Mt. Goddard. The next day I would be meeting friends down below at McGee Lakes, but for that final night I was alone in one of the most magnificent places on earth. I arrived on top in the late afternoon amidst threatening skies. I had been worried that I would be thirsty on top, since I only had a one quart water bottle with me, but when the sun was out I was able to melt snow on the dark fabric of my pack cloth, and there was also an occasional shower allowing me to collect water off my bright red

tarp (see photo below). Setting up a tarp on top of a mountain with no trees in sight is a challenge, but I anchored it securely to rocks I stacked, hoping fervently that the conditions didn't get worse. I didn't want to be on top if there were lightning or a major storm. I debated going down, but then decided to stay. I was glad I did.

One doesn't usually expect to see much wildlife on top of a mountain, but as I was enjoying the spectacular sunset, a golden eagle soared by, floating on the thermals. In seconds he was just a far-off speck, but I gave a whistle, and he made a sharp turn and came back. He stayed around for almost five minutes as I periodically whistled. It was a magical time, sharing the summit and the beautiful sky with one of God's wild creatures. My

journal records the following inscription that night, "Another glorious day has passed in the mountains. Thank you, God for sharing the wonders of this day with me. Oh, that I might be able to stay up here forever!"

When I contemplate "forever," I think of a short parable of a bird and a mountain that Hendrik Willem Van Loon once wrote:

People – Day Six of Creation

Then God said, "Let us make man in our image." …And there was evening, and there was morning – the sixth day. Genesis 1:24-31

After each of the first five days of creation, the Scriptures record the refrain, "And God saw that it was good." But on the sixth day we find something which God says is *not* good – it is not good that man is without a suitable partner. And so God performs one final creative act and creates woman from man's rib. At this point, the creation is complete, and the Scriptures declare a slightly modified refrain: "God saw all that he had made, and it was very good" (Genesis 1:31).

God created millions of species of sea creatures, birds and land animals, but man was unique in a special way. For God made man in his own image. We probably won't fully understand what this means until we see God face to face. Then, free from the tarnishing effect of sin, it will become clear how our thoughts reflect his thoughts, how our feelings are like his feelings, how the way we relate to others is a reflection of how he also communicates. After creating man from the dust of the earth and breathing into him the breath of life, God blessed him and gave him dominion over all the earth, telling him to "rule over the fish of the sea and the birds of the air and over every living creature that moves on the ground" (Genesis 1:28). Being in a position of authority is another way in which we bear

> The amazing way in which God knit together the human body is a center-stage example of God's artistic ability

God's image, though he rules over a far greater territory!

God placed man in the Garden of Eden "to work it and take care of it" (Genesis 2:15). Reconciling these dual tasks has been man's challenge throughout the ages: using creation, but not abusing it. Conservation efforts have gained momentum in recent times because man has been lax in fulfilling his responsibility to take care of the earth.

In their book *Fearfully and Wonderfully Made*, Philip Yancey and Paul Brand explore how intricately God created the human body. The various structures and systems that work together to keep us alive are nothing short of miraculous: the protection of our skin, the strength of our bones, the dynamic motion of our muscles, the energy of our heart, the response of our immune system, the cognitive ability of our brain … the list goes on and on. The amazing way in which God knit together the human body is a center-stage example of God's artistic ability.

When God first made man, he and man fellowshipped regularly in the Garden of Eden. This is something which God sought out, coming to talk with Adam and Eve in the cool of the day. But then that fellowship was broken. Man disobeyed God, death entered the world, and those who bore the marks of sin were sent away from the presence of a holy God. God waited thousands of years before supplying a definitive solution, long enough for man to realize that he could never pay for his sin on his own, or make himself holy enough to come back into God's presence. Then

God provided a bridge to span the chasm. He sent his own Son to become a man, and this one succeeded where all others had failed: he lived a holy, sinless life.

Satan had been trying to kill the Son since the time of the Son's birth, or to tempt him to sin as he had done with Adam. Still seething after being thrown out of heaven, Satan thought that the way he could hurt God most was to kill God's own dear Son. And so Satan entered into a friend of the Son, Judas Iscariot, who then betrayed the Son. The Son was tortured and killed in the cruelest manner possible. Satan appeared to be victorious as the Son's followers dispersed and hid behind locked doors.

But there were several things that Satan didn't know at the time of his apparent victory. The first was that the Son had the power to come back from the grave. And so three days after his death, ***Jesus*** came back to life and appeared to his friends. The second thing Satan didn't know is described by C.S. Lewis in his allegorical book, *The Lion, the Witch and the Wardrobe*: "When a willing victim who had committed no treachery was killed in a traitor's stead … then Death itself would start working backwards." The life of a sinless man had been given in exchange for the sin of the entire human race, and now that sin's penalty had been paid in full, the curse of death could be lifted.

> Sinful man can now become sinless in God's sight by having all his sin paid for by Christ's atoning sacrifice

The door to God was now open. The curtain separating a holy God from a sinful man was now rent in two. God had provided access for man to be reconciled with him, to have renewed fellowship with him. Sinful man could now become sinless in God's sight by having all his sin paid for by Christ's atoning sacrifice. To those who accept the Son, who believe in him, their sin is taken away, and they can enter into the presence of a holy God. And not only that, but God adopts them as his children so that they are part of his family.

The story of the Bible is primarily a story of redemption. Those who have found reconciliation with God are enjoined to make known this reconciliation to the ends of the earth. And so the story goes out to the peoples of the world. The Holy Spirit provided the model for this effort, miraculously causing the first believers he came upon to glorify God in a variety of different languages. *The Ethnologue* catalogues 6,912 unique ethnic groups in the world today, each with a different language. Following the example of John Wycliffe, who first translated the Bible into English, missionaries and nationals are working together to translate the good news for those inhabiting the farthest corners of the earth. Jesus said, "This gospel of the kingdom will be preached in the whole world as a testimony to all nations (*ethnē* in Greek – all ethnic groups), and then the end will come" (Matthew 24:14). We are surely in the last days as the word goes out to all the world.

A little Sunday School rhyme talks of how God loves all the children he has made: "red and yellow, black and white, they are precious in his sight." God's chosen are not only precious to him, they are destined to be his bride. The prophet Isaiah tells us that "as a bridegroom rejoices over his bride, so will your God rejoice over you" (Isaiah 62:5). The image of a bride is a beautiful picture showing God's desire to love and have fellowship with those he died to redeem.

What hope we have, to live forever with our Creator, and to enjoy fellowship with him beyond the boundaries of time. We are the final brush stroke in the present canvas, but God is currently at work on another canvas, creating a new heaven and a new earth. As we walk with our Maker, we will have the privilege to appreciate that one as well.

"Let the heavens rejoice, let the earth be glad; let them say among the nations, 'The Lord reigns!'"   *(1 Chronicles 16:31)*

"As high as the heavens are above the earth, so great is his love for those who fear him."   *(Psalm 103:11)*

"God is love: He shall wipe away creation's tears, and all the worlds shall summer in his smile." *Alexander Smith*

"If one advances confidently in the direction of one's dreams, and endeavors to live the life which he has imagined, he will meet with a success unexpected in common hours."   *Henry David Thoreau*

"True glory consists in doing what deserves to be written; in writing what deserves to be read; and in so living as to make the world happier for our living in it." *Pliny the Elder*

"For God, who said, "Let light shine out of darkness," made his light shine in our hearts…"   *(2 Corinthians 4:6)*

"What people say you can not do, you try and find you can." *Henry David Thoreau*

"All humanity finds shelter in the shadow of your wings."   *(Psalm 36:7)*

"Love is a canvas furnished by Nature and embroidered by imagination." *Voltaire*

"Go confidently in the direction of your dreams! Live the life you've imagined."   *Henry David Thoreau*

"But you are a chosen people … that you may declare the praises
of him who called you out of darkness into his wonderful light." *(1 Peter 2:9)*

Interaction with the Creator – The Bearers of God's Image

In our work overseas as missionaries, we once experienced both the best and the worst in man, all in the space of an hour. It happened on the day we left the village for the final time. For ten years my wife Laura and I had been living with the Kwatay people of Senegal in the village of Diembering. Their language had never been written before, so we learned the language, developed an alphabet, and then produced a body of literature including primers, a dictionary, and booklets on health, community development, local folk stories, as well as stories from the Bible. Life there was not easy – our family lived in a mud brick house with no electricity or running water, and we often fell sick with malaria and other tropical diseases. But God was good, and with his help, we worked with the nationals to produce the New Testament in the Kwatay language, a large book of stories from the Old Testament, as well as the JESUS Film.

We had developed some close friendships with the people, and our two children had basically lived there their whole lives. So the day of our departure was a difficult, emotional time. The group of believers gathered at our house to say good-bye. Before leaving, one of the elders suggested we have a time of prayer. I sat next to Jean-Paul who had just recently become a believer. Several weeks before he had pulled me aside and said, "I want to wait until after you leave to be baptized. Then people will know I'm not just doing it because of your influence, but because I truly believe." As I sat praying next to Jean-Paul, I opened my eyes, and I could see drops of water making big splotches on the cement below him. They were teardrops of sadness and love. In a culture where men don't cry, those tears spoke volumes. The pastor closed the time of prayer by asking God himself to accompany us as we left and drove through rebel infested jungle to reach the capital. "Don't just send an angel to watch over them," he prayed, "but just as you yourself accompanied the children of Israel into the desert, go with Steve and Laura, Nika and Kevin."

As we drove away from the village we were filled with a spirit of rejoicing and thankfulness for all that God had accomplished in our years with the Kwatay. The believers were still few in number, but they were strong in their faith, the church was growing, and they had the Word of God in a language they could understand. We drove down the dirt track

thanking God for each of the precious friends we were leaving behind. They had shown us such love – they were an example of man at his best, man truly reflecting God's image.

It was not long before we met man at his worst. As we drove down the one road that connected our village to the city about 90 minutes away, a man stepped out from the side of the road to flag us down. This was not unusual since people often want a ride and there are few vehicles. But the pickup we had borrowed from another missionary was full that day with all our belongings, so I started to pass on by. The man was turned sideways, waving me to stop with his left hand. What I didn't see was that in his right hand he had a rifle. As the truck started to pass, he took a step back and then brought up his gun, spraying the truck with automatic weapon fire.

Miraculously God protected our family. We later found a bullet that had passed just under the kids and was lodged in the gas tank –

thankfully for us our friend's truck was a diesel and therefore it didn't explode. Other bullets hit the truck as well, with one passing within inches of Laura's head before splintering the front windshield. As I realized what was taking place I hit the brakes, knowing the rebel would continue fir-

ing if I kept going, and knowing I could never outrun another hail of bullets.

As we skidded to a stop the man ran up to the passenger window, threatening us with his AK47 and yelling, "Give me your money." He had a wild, crazed look in his eye. We had a lot of money with us since we had just sold all our furniture and appliances. And we also had a fair bit of cash left over from a village-wide celebration we had hosted for the dedication of the New Testament, at which we'd fed 3,500 people. I had put the money in two places. The first was in a sock that also contained the flash to my camera. The man took the sock, but was so distracted watching the road to make sure an army vehicle wasn't approaching that he didn't realize there was money beneath the flash. He came back to the car threatening us more violently, "Give me your money!" Laura was fumbling in our backpack for the other packet of money when the man saw the camera gear in the backpack. He reached through the window and grabbed the whole backpack. Besides the camera, lenses and video camera, all our pictures and the video of the dedication ceremony were in that backpack, along with pictures we'd taken of our friends before leaving – my heart tore in two as I saw them all disappear out the window. But after just a few seconds the man was back again, and this time he was even more angry. "Give me your money!" he screamed. I calmly told him that he already had all our money, and that if he would permit me I would get out of the truck and show him where it was. He motioned for me to go ahead. With my arms raised, I got out and went over to the side of the road, took the money out of the sock and showed it to him. Then for some reason I asked if we could have our passports and papers back, since they wouldn't do him any good. The man called out to another rebel I had not seen previously who was covering us from the edge of the jungle. He said the backpack with our papers was over there and we must go over and talk to the other guy to get the passports back. But as I started to approach, the other man took out a long knife. I told the first man I couldn't go over there because I was afraid of the knife.

At that instant, another car approached, and the first rebel went back out on the road to force it to stop as well. He once again brandished his weapon and demanded money. A woman in the back seat leaned out to give him some, but when he leaned over to take it from her, he saw that the passenger in the front was a man in military fatigues who had a rifle. The soldier couldn't turn the rifle around in the small car to point it the other way, and so the rebel reached in through the front window and tried to take it. The man resisted. The rebel then stepped back and sprayed the car with a long burst of fire. I was standing on the road perhaps twenty feet away, and when the shooting started I ran for the pickup and hid on the far side.

With all our belongings in the pickup, Laura and the kids couldn't see out the back, and they didn't know another car had arrived on the scene. They only knew I was back there somewhere, and when they heard the firing, they assumed I had been shot. I looked out from the side of the pickup and could see the rebels picking up the stuff they had taken from us and fleeing into the bush. Laura and the kids were surprised to see me. They were afraid and urged me to get in the truck so we could leave. But first I had to go back and see if anyone in the other car had survived. There was only silence; it was not a pretty sight. I ran back to the pickup and we took off, continuing on through the jungle. Not too long later we arrived at a military checkpoint where we explained to the captain what had happened, and he closed the road and sent soldiers back to secure the area.

In the space of an hour, we had gone from seeing man at his best to seeing man at his worst. We had gone out from the presence of friends who would have laid down their lives for us, into the presence of people who didn't care a whit whether we lived or died.

Man was originally created in God's image – that is why even those who don't acknowledge God are capable of doing good. But as a result of the fall, man is also prone to commit evil. And it is that evil, whether large or small, which separates us from an infinitely holy God. One day those of us who have accepted the offer Jesus made to pay for our evil will have it removed. We will be given new bodies that aren't imprinted with the sin nature or the consequences of that first sin. No longer will God's image be marred by man's evil. No longer will the flesh and the spirit be at war in our bodies. On that day we will once again be as God originally intended for us to be. We will be in his image, free from all trace of sin. What a day that will be!

Resting – Day Seven of Creation

After working six days, God finished creating the universe and everything in it, and on the seventh day he rested. It was not that God was tired or taxed by his work and in need of a break; he was simply done with the task of creating new things. When God rested on the seventh day he set an example for man to follow. God knew that man would be driven by a desire for progress, a desire to build, to work, to get ahead. Work is not bad, but we can be so intent on forging ahead that other valuable things are crowded out. When we rest there is time for families and picnics. There is time for a stroll in the woods or a Sunday drive. There is time to appreciate what God created in his six days of work, and time to reflect on our own work of the prior six days. And there is time to join with others of faith to worship God.

> The wonderful thing about a day of rest is that it allows us to forget our worries and just enjoy life

The Scriptures say that God blessed the seventh day and made it holy, thereby establishing a principle that those who set apart that day for God would partake of the blessing. We are tempted to think that we can make more progress by working on the seventh day rather than resting, but normal laws do not apply when it comes to the day that God set apart as holy. When the children of Israel escaped Egypt and fled into the wilderness, they became hungry and cried out to God for food. God gave them manna to eat. Normally the manna was just good for one day; when some tried to save it overnight it developed maggots. God wanted his people to learn to look to him for their daily food. After giving the Israelites manna for five days, God told them that on the sixth day they were to collect twice as much, so that they could take the seventh day as "a day of rest, a holy Sabbath to the Lord" (Exodus 16:23). And a miracle took place that seventh day: the same manna, which had previously developed maggots when kept overnight, was perfectly fine when it was kept for the Sabbath day. God temporarily changed the natural order of things because he had put a special blessing on the Sabbath day, making it holy.

It is often difficult for us to see the seventh day as being any different from the other six days. The Israelites also had a problem with this. God provided them with enough manna on day six so that they wouldn't have to collect any more on day seven. But that first Sabbath, some people still went out to find more. Perhaps when they saw that the manna they'd gathered the day before hadn't spoiled, they thought they could get ahead by working to get additional manna. But they soon discovered that there wasn't any more to gather on day seven. For that one day God cut off the supply. And herein lies another principle: those who would work on the Sabbath to get further ahead are not making any real progress. In the light of eternity they are coming up empty handed, because it is only when we follow the way God has established that we'll be blessed.

The wonderful thing about a day of rest is that it allows us to forget our worries and just enjoy life. It is a sign that we are trusting God to feed us, to clothe us, to house us. We tend to think it is up to us to provide the basic necessities of life for ourselves, but truly it is God who gives us our daily bread and everything else we require. When we recognize that God is our provider, then we are truly able to rest on the seventh day. Rest does not mean doing nothing at all, it is rather a cessation of the normal work by which we make our living. Mowing the lawn on Sunday isn't an issue, unless you run a gardening business the other six days of the week! Neither is washing the car, or fixing things around the house. But we should be careful lest the day of rest becomes just another busy day of work on personal matters. Part of the reason God created the Sabbath was so that we would have time for him! God wants our fellowship, our worship. On the seventh day we have time to join with other believers to corporately worship God and to learn from his Word. We have time for a prayer walk in the woods to talk to God about how our lives are going, to thank him for all he's done for us, and to ask him for his help.

The principle that God will bless man when he rests is difficult to grasp, so God gave the children of Israel another example, in addition to the double provision of manna on the sixth day. For six years they were to work the ground, but the seventh was to be a year of Sabbath rest – a year of celebration in which they were not to do any work in the fields. What a matter of trust! Back then, their sustenance came completely from their fields. But because God had blessed the seventh year and considered it holy, he caused the fields to flourish and produce without anyone ever

> A day of rest gives us time to reflect on all God has wrought, both in the world and in our lives

planting or weeding or watering. And so for one whole year the people were able to rest and rejoice in God's provision.

The principle of resting is more important than the day on which it is done. Some people today rest on Saturday, the 7th day of the week; others consider Sunday to be their Sabbath day of rest; still others must work the weekend and they take off a weekday. Paul addressed this issue in Romans 14:5. He didn't require all believers to observe one specific day, but rather he said, "One man considers one day more sacred than another; another man considers every day alike. Each one should be fully convinced in his own mind." In Christ we are free to choose the day, but the principle established since creation is that we should take time to rest in honor of God.

When we consider the day of rest, we should see it as a day of opportunity and celebration. What an amazing thing to be given time to play, to reflect, to worship. Life's clock ticks by all too quickly, and before we know it the seventy-odd years we are allotted are over. The day of rest gives us a chance to slow down and do those things which are really important in the overall scheme of things. This is the way we can arrive at the end of our lives with no regrets. The Argentine writer Jorge Luis Borges spoke of regrets when he penned his last poem, entitled *Moments*, shortly before dying. Here are a few of the moments he wished he could recapture:

If I could live my life over again … I would laugh more…
I would take more risks and go on more trips;
I would watch more sunsets, climb more mountains, swim more rivers.
I would go to more places I have never been,
eat more ice cream and fewer lima beans.
I would have more real problems
and fewer imaginary ones…

If I could live again, I'd travel more lightly…
I would walk around barefoot from the
beginning of spring until the end of autumn.
I would take more spins on the merry-go-round,
contemplate more sunrises and play with more children –
if I had another life to live.
But you see, I'm 85 years old, and I'm dying.

When we experience the blessing God has reserved for those who rest, we can arrive at the end of our lives without regret. We've taken the time to do all those things that, in the end, were really important. We might not have become wealthy or famous, but we have memories that no amount of money can buy.

When we look at the Creator's canvas, we tend to look at what God did on just the first six days of creation. But the seventh day is a part of the masterpiece as well. The number seven is a symbol of perfection in the Scriptures, and in fact, the creation is only perfect when it includes day seven. How our Maker is worthy of praise – he who did such wonders that week when the world first began, and who continues week by week to do the same!

"I will … reflect on your ways."   *(Psalm 119:15, NLT)*

"There is a way that nature speaks, that land speaks.
Most of the time we are simply not patient enough, quiet enough, to pay attention to the story." *Linda Hogan*

"The question is not what you look at, but what you see." *Henry David Thoreau*

"All we have to decide is what to do with the time that is given to us."   *J.R.R. Tolkein*

"Short is the little time which remains to thee of life. Live as on a mountain."   *Marcus Aurelius*

"All I have seen teaches me to trust the Creator for all I have not seen."   *Ralph Waldo Emerson*

"Praise the Lord, everything he has created, everywhere in his kingdom."   *(Psalm 103:22, NLT)*

About the Photos

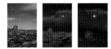

Cover. Burned Timber Trail, Taylor Creek, Oregon. Taken November 6, 2004. F 2.8, 1/60th second, 38mm. The sun was just starting to burn through the fog as I topped a ridge, creating a special "God moment." The rays lasted only a few minutes and then the fog lifted and the sky was blue.

Page 7. Crater Lake, Oregon. Taken May 12, 2007. F 5, various shutter speeds, 19mm. I skied up and slept on top of The Watchman at the edge of Crater Lake and woke up to take this panorama of the sunrise at 5:50 a.m. The photo is composed of three shots taken with a wide-angle lens on a tripod, and each of the shots were exposed three times using auto-exposure bracketing, and then combined using the High Dynamic Range (HDR) software package Photomatix.

Page 11. South Jetty County Park, Bandon, Oregon. Taken October 16, 2006. F 8, 1/60th second, 70mm. When I saw the shaft of light coming through the arch I ran down the hill to the beach. I only had time to capture this one image and then the sun dropped behind a cloud and the shaft of light disappeared. I was bemoaning my bad luck, because I easily could have taken a lot more photos from different angles, but in the end, I was thankful for the one shot I did get.

Page 12. Upper Table Rock, Medford, Oregon. Taken December 10, 2005. F 6.3, 1/500th second, 94mm. The winter sun was low in the sky and it cast a long shadow off a tall tree on the ridge as it burned through the fog.

Page 13. Mt. Thielsen, Oregon. Taken September 30, 2006. F 13, 1/80th second, 216mm. I spent the night on top of Mt. Bailey and caught the sun just as it broke the horizon. Smoke from nearby forest fires colored the horizon orange, while the sky above was purple and blue.

Page 14. Burned Timber Trail, Taylor Creek, Oregon. Taken November 6, 2004. Both photos at F 2.8, 1/125th second, 38mm. The sun was just burning through the morning fog, causing rays of light to filter down through the forest of old-growth Douglas Fir.

Page 15. Looking north from Sandy Saddle on Mt. McLoughlin, Oregon. Taken August 18, 2007. F 11, various shutter speeds, 85m. Low lying fog turns pink as the sun rises over the Cascades. In the distance from left to right are Union Peak, Mt. Bailey, Mt. Thielsen, and Mt. Scott. The photo is composed of three shots taken on a tripod with auto-exposure bracketing, and then combined using the High Dynamic Range (HDR) software package Photomatix.

Page 16. Harris State Beach, Brookings, Oregon. Taken November 24, 2006. F 9, 1/200th second, 45mm. It had been a wet, stormy day, but it cleared up a bit in the late afternoon, providing a spectacular sunset.

Page 17. Arua, Uganda. Taken August 28, 2006. F 6.3, 1/100th second, 112mm. Seeing a brilliant rainbow against the dark sky behind the cathedral, I grabbed my camera and ran about a quarter mile to where I would get an unobstructed view. By the time I arrived the rainbow had faded, but the soft afternoon light brought the front of the cathedral out in sharp contrast with the dark storm clouds in the background.

Page 21. Lake Shastina, California. Taken July 26, 1982. Exposure not recorded, Kodachrome 64 slide film. With the afternoon wind on Lake Shastina there was no chance for a smooth reflection, but the sun setting over the Eddies resulted in spectacular colors in the sky.

Page 22. Summit of Mt. Whitney, California. Taken August 2, 1980. Exposures not recorded, Kodachrome 64 slide film. The series of shots was taken as the sun set in a fiery red display, causing an ever increasing alpenglow on the stone hut on the summit of Mt. Whitney. A group of us spent a somewhat cold but thoroughly enjoyable night on top of the highest peak in the lower 48 states.

Page 23. Fish Lake, Oregon. Taken March 11, 2006. F 18, 1/500th second, 28mm. I had just finished a cross country ski outing and was back at the car when the sun broke through the clouds for the first time that day. The snow had been sticking terribly to my skis, but I put them back on, slogged down to the shore of the lake, and was rewarded with a beautiful view.

Page 24. Cathedral Peak, Yosemite, California. Taken August 1, 1984. Exposure not recorded, Kodachrome 64 slide film. Looking back at Cathedral Peak, which I had climbed earlier that morning, the clouds towering over it made me wish Ansel Adams could have been beside me with his large format black and white camera.
Page 24. Clarence King, Kings Canyon National Park. Taken July 23, 1979. Exposure not recorded, Kodachrome 64 slide film. A "sun dog" (a kind of rainbow known technically as a *parhelion*) appeared briefly in the sky while we were on top of Mt. Clarence King, adding just a bit more color to an already spectacular view.

Page 25. Grayback Mountain, Oregon. Taken June 30, 2006. F 5.6, 1/125th second, 216mm. I spent a night sleeping on top of Grayback Mountain, the highest peak in Josephine County, and was treated to a fiery red sky as the sun set over the coastal range.

Page 26. Lake above Wallace Creek, Sequoia National Park, California. Taken July 27, 1980. Exposure not recorded, Kodachrome 64 slide film. As the sun set I could see individual trees reflected in the lake, whereas when I looked at the shore they just blended into the dark ridge.
Page 26. Lake by Finger Peak, Kings Canyon National Park, California. Taken August 5, 1979. Exposure not recorded, Kodachrome 64 slide film. The last rays of alpenglow were hitting the distant peaks and clouds as the sun set. I was on an 11 day solo backpack, miles from the nearest trail, but after this display I knew I wasn't alone!

Page 27. Arua, Uganda. Taken May 19, 2006. F 7.1, 1/200th second, 216mm. As I was walking through the rural countryside, a thunderhead building in the late afternoon sky caught my attention. It was just starting to catch the first colors of the sunset.

Page 28. Between Juneau and Ketchikan, Alaska. Taken August 13, 2004. F 4.5, 1/500th second, 59mm. We were traveling through the calm waters of the Inner Passage when I saw this wisp of cloud, and it seemed like a brush stroke God was painting on an open expanse of sky.

Page 29. Yosemite Valley, California. Taken January 1, 1987. Exposure not recorded, Kodachrome 64 slide film. The moon was rising over a new dusting of snow on Half Dome as the sun set. It was a wonderful way to watch the first day of 1987 draw to a close.

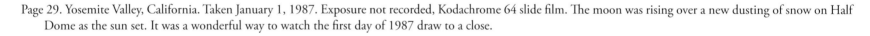

Page 30. Royal Arches, Yosemite, California. Taken July, 1984. Exposure not recorded, Kodachrome 64 slide Film. One summer afternoon, three of us climbed "Serenity Crack" on Royal Arches, a 5.10d.

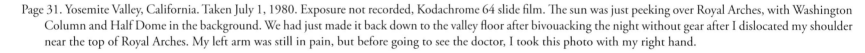

Page 31. Yosemite Valley, California. Taken July 1, 1980. Exposure not recorded, Kodachrome 64 slide film. The sun was just peeking over Royal Arches, with Washington Column and Half Dome in the background. We had just made it back down to the valley floor after bivouacking the night without gear after I dislocated my shoulder near the top of Royal Arches. My left arm was still in pain, but before going to see the doctor, I took this photo with my right hand.

Page 34. Shastina, California. Taken January 22, 2006. F 6.3, 1/750th second, 209mm. Snow plumes were blowing off the top of Shastina on this blustery winter morning as the sun came over the top of Mt. Shasta, which can be seen rising just to the right of Shastina. Fog in the foreground added a feeling of mystery to the scene.

Page 35. Elliot Glacier, Mt. Hood, Oregon. Taken September 1, 1984. Exposure not recorded, Kodachrome 64 slide film. An unsuccessful attempt by Eric Spangenberg and I to climb the North side of Mt. Hood almost took on epic proportions as we rappelled off an ice bollard and made our way back down through the crevasse field after dark without headlamps. After 18 hours on the mountain we made it back to the car at midnight.
Page 35. Peak 8,913 ft. Trinity Alps, California. Taken June, 1982. Exposure not recorded, Kodachrome 64 slide film. The clouds partly hiding the sheer face of the peak gave it a sense of mystery.

Page 36. Mt. Thielsen from Mt. Bailey, Oregon. Taken September 30, 2006. F 13, 2.5 seconds, 56mm. Just below the summit of Mt. Bailey is an 8 foot high "window" in the rock ridge, and I captured the first hints of color through it as the sun prepared to rise over Mt. Thielsen.

Page 37. Denali National Park, Alaska. Taken August 8, 2004. F 3.2, 1/500th second, 189mm. The shot was taken at about 5 in the morning, but being so far north in summer it was already day! Morning fog still hung over the river, while above it rose the Denali range, just to the east of Mt. McKinley.

Page 38. The Matterhorn, Switzerland. Taken April, 1990. Exposure not recorded, Kodachrome 64 slide film. Fresh snow on the Matterhorn stands in sharp contrast with a deep blue sky.

Page 38. Window Peak, Kings Canyon National Park, California. Taken July 26, 1979. Exposure not recorded, Kodachrome 64 slide film. Just below the summit of Window Peak is a large window in the granite that can even be seen from the lake fourteen hundred feet below.

Page 39. Shastina, California. Taken January 22, 2006. F 5, 1/750th second, 317mm. This shot of Shastina was taken from Lake Shastina on the north side of the mountain, just as the first alpenglow was starting to light the peak. The summit of Mt. Shasta can just be seen peeking through the clouds.

Page 40. Ridge by Watchman Overlook, Crater Lake, Oregon. Taken January 22, 2007. F 10, 1/320th second, 96mm. The late afternoon sun was catching just the top of the ridges on the inside edge of the crater. Several full size trees can be seen in the photo, and they testify to the immense size of the snow covered ridges.

Page 41. Mt. Hood, Oregon. Taken May 1, 1984. Exposure not recorded, Kodachrome 64 slide film. We climbed the difficult Leuthold Couloir on Mt. Hood, arriving at this ridge just below the summit. As soon as we got to the top of Mt. Hood the clouds descended in a white out. We blindly made our way down the standard route on the south side, and after 500 feet we caught up to a party that had just turned around due to the weather. They had put out wands to mark their route, and we were able to follow the wands all the way back down.

Page 42. Mt. Thielsen from the top of The Watchman, Crater Lake, Oregon. Taken May 11, 2007. F 5.6, 1/320th second, 288mm. The sun had already set inside the rim at Crater Lake, but was still hitting the top of Mt. Thielsen.

Page 43. Fourmile Lake from Mt. McLoughlin, Oregon. Taken June 29, 2005. F 6.3, 1/500th second, 139mm. My wife Laura on an outcrop of rock just below the summit of Mt. McLoughlin.

Page 44. Crater Lake, Oregon. Taken January 22, 2007. F 11, 1/60th second, 60mm. I was snow camping on the edge of Crater Lake, just beyond Discovery Point, and as the sun rose the first rays hit the edge of the crater and were reflected in the areas of the lake which hadn't been covered in skim ice from the cold night air. Part of Wizard Island can be seen in the lake at the right.

Page 45. Cascade Range from the Middle Sister, Oregon. Taken July 1, 1982. Exposure not recorded, Kodachrome 64 slide film. I spent the night on top of Middle Sister and took this shot looking north. A line of volcanoes appear through the evening haze of nearby forest fires: Mt. Washington, Three Fingered Jack, Mt. Jefferson, Mt. Hood, and Mt. St. Helens.

Page 46. Mt. Foraker, Alaska. Taken August 9, 2004. F 3.7, 1/125th second, 380mm. Sunset in Alaska in the middle of summer happens just before 11 p.m.! The shot was taken from the grounds of the Mt. McKinley Wilderness Lodge. The layers of different colored peaks give the photo a sense of depth.

Page 47. Chiore River, Bolivia. Taken November, 1983. Exposure not recorded, Kodachrome 64 slide film. In an attempt to make a friendly contact with the Yuqui tribe in the Amazon jungle of Bolivia, we hung gifts of bananas and machetes across their jungle trails. Steve Parker, who is seated just behind the man hanging bananas, was later speared by a Yuqui, but he lived and was later able to share the gospel with them.

Page 47. Huayana Potosi, Bolivia. Taken November, 1983. Exposure not recorded, Kodachrome 64 slide film. Preparing to leave basecamp at 18,700 feet for our summit bid, this shot was taken in the early morning, long before sunrise.

Page 48. Huayana Potosi, Bolivia. Taken November, 1983. Exposure not recorded, Kodachrome 64 slide film. Myself on the summit of Huayana Potosi, breathing that much sought after 20,000 foot air.

Page 50. South County Jetty Park, Bandon, Oregon. Taken October 16, 2006. F 5.6, 1/125th second, 174mm. A couple and their dog prepare to watch the sunset from a point overlooking majestic rock outcroppings on the Oregon coast.

Page 51. Florence, Oregon. Taken October 15, 2006. F 5, 1/60th second, 56mm. Hundreds of sanderlings gathered to search for an evening meal in the sand as the sun sank into the sea.

Page 52. Harris State Beach, Brookings, Oregon. Taken March 24, 2005. F 3.5, 1/350th second, 337mm. The waves, rocks, clouds and sky provided a variety of layers as the sun set in a spectacular display.

Page 53. Face Rock State Scenic Viewpoint, Bandon, Oregon. Taken October 16, 2006. F 11, 1/500th second, 120mm. Rocks sculpted by the ocean into various shapes provided an interesting backdrop as a couple walked the beach. The shot was taken just before sunset.

Page 54. Harris State Beach, Brookings, Oregon. Taken March 24, 2005. F 7, 1/1500th second, 380mm. My son Kevin braves the cold water of the Pacific Ocean in early spring. The sun broke through the clouds for just a short time, but even though the air was cold and the water was colder, he was determined to get in!

Page 55. Gold Beach, Oregon. Taken November 25, 2005. F 3.2, 1/250th second, 117mm. Clumps of sea grass blowing in the wind provide a soft foreground for this beach scene.

Page 56. Harris State Beach, Brookings, Oregon. Taken March 24, 2005. F 4.5, 1/500th second, 128mm. The bright heavens in contrast with the darker earth seemed a fitting statement on the glory of God and the world's need for light and redemption.

Page 57. Heceta Head Lighthouse, Oregon. Taken October 16, 2006. F 7.1, 1/125th second, 52mm. The cove and waves lead the eye to the lighthouse on the point, which flashed just as I released the shutter.

Page 58. Gold Beach, Oregon. Taken November 26, 2005. F 8, 1/8th second, 337mm. I was down at the beach before sunrise when I saw this scene. Not having a tripod with me, I placed the camera on a large tree trunk in the sand and set the self timer. The tide was coming in, and I had to grab the camera and run several times before there was enough of a lull in the approaching waves to be able to set up and take the shot without getting soaked.

Page 59. Gold Beach, Oregon. Taken November 25, 2005. F 5, 1/500th second, 380mm. A strong offshore wind blows misty spray off the line of backlit breakers as the sun starts to set.

Page 60. Gold Beach, Oregon. Taken November 25, 2005. F 3.5, 1/250th second, 307mm. A small private lookout in the shape of a lighthouse provides a scenic spot for the owner to watch the sunset.

Page 61. Harris State Beach, Brookings, Oregon. Taken March 24, 2005. F 6.3, 1/500th second, 105mm. My son Kevin enjoys the sunset reflecting in the surf.

Page 62. Hideaway Island, Efate, Vanuatu. Taken 2002. Exposure not recorded, Kodak 100 Gold film. My son Kevin and I in the crystal clear water of the Marine Preserve at Hideaway Island. Photo taken by my wife Laura.

Page 63. Vanuatu. December 27, 2002. An image of Cyclone Zoe from the US Navy's Joint Typhoon Warning Center website. Vanuatu is made up of numerous islands, seen in green at the bottom left edge of the cyclone. Cyclone Zoe is described on the Wikipedia website as the most intense tropical cyclone ever observed in the Southern Hemisphere. The cyclone had been heading directly toward us, but just as it started to hit the islands it changed direction 120 degrees and we were saved.

Page 66. South, Middle and North Sister, from Golden Lake, Oregon. Taken August 9, 2007. F 7.1, 1/125th second, 45mm. Middle and North Sister are reflected in Golden Lake at sunrise. The photo is actually composed of four photos which were stitched together to form a panorama. Shortly after the photos were taken the wind came up and the reflection could no longer be seen.

Page 67. Crater Lake, Oregon. Taken January 22, 2007. F 11, 1/4th second, 45mm. I cross country skied to Discovery Point and camped right on the rim of the crater. I set my alarm so that I'd be up for the first rays of the sunrise. It was a frigid 17 degrees, and getting out of my warm sleeping bag was a challenge, but once I saw the reflection of Wizard Island and the cliffs I knew I had made the right decision!

Page 68. Lake Damariscotta, Maine. Taken August, 1997. Exposure not recorded, Kodak Gold 100 film. My father-in-law and his brother took a rowboat out on Lake Damariscotta for some early morning bass fishing. The night was cold and steam was coming off the water as the sun rose and colored the water with a beautiful golden hue.

Page 69. Romona Falls, Mt. Hood. Taken August 5, 2006. F 14, 6 seconds, 48mm. I spent five days hiking the Timberline Trail which circumnavigates Mt. Hood, and camping by this waterfall was one of the highlights. I didn't have a tripod, so I leveled the camera on a tree, set the self timer, and took the long exposure.

Page 70. Taylor Creek, Oregon. Taken February 3, 2007. F 11, 1/6th second, 53mm. A cold snap caused icicles to form on a log just above the little falls. The photo blends both movement and stability, and the triangular composition leads the eye to the focal point.

Page 71. Yellowstone Falls, Wyoming. Taken July, 1988. Exposure not recorded, Kodachrome 64 slide film. Backlighting on the spray from the late afternoon sun and the reflection of the snaking river help convey a sense of the majesty of these magnicient falls.
Page 71. National Creek Falls, Oregon. Taken September 30, 2006. F 29, 1/6th second, 85mm. The water follows several paths down the cliff, some cascading straight down, some following the stairsteps in the rock, and some spilling down the log.

Page 72. Lake Damariscotta, Maine. Taken June 30, 2007. F 11, 1/13th second, 45mm. Early morning fog rises from the lake as the sun promises to shortly make an appearance. The shot was taken at 5:13 a.m. using a graduated neutral density filter.

Page 73. Middle Fowler Falls, McCloud, California. Taken July 25, 2004. F 4.5, 1/500th second, 105mm. My daughter Nika contemplates the falls before diving into the pool at their base. The water in the McCloud river comes down from Mt. Shasta in underground lava tubes, and even on a hot summer day the water is in the low 40's.

Page 74. Junction Meadow, Kern River, Sequoia National Park, California. Taken August, 1980. Exposure not recorded, Kodachrome 64 slide film. Water in Junction Meadow quietly flows over a knot on a log.

Page 75. National Creek Falls, Oregon. Taken September 30, 2006. F 29, 1/6th second, 120mm. Beams of afternoon sun filtering through the trees light up the vegetation beside National Creek Falls.

Page 76. Rainey Falls, Rogue River, Galice, Oregon. Taken May 29, 2004. F 4.5, 1/750th second, 189mm. A rafter stands and braces himself as he goes over Rainey Falls, a class 5 rapid. There is actually another person in the front of the raft, and though he is invisible behind a wall of spray, his paddle can be clearly seen!

Page 77. Iceland Lake, Emigrant Wilderness, California. Taken August 8, 2005. F 2.8, 1/180th second, 40mm. Evening alpenglow lights up the rocks around this lake in the high Sierras.

Page 78. Green Creek, Yosemite, California. Taken August, 1982. Exposure not recorded, Kodachrome 64 slide film. As a guide with Sierra Treks, I set up this Tyrolean traverse across the gorge to give the students a bit of excitement!
Page 78. South Fork of the Kings River, Kings Canyon National Park, California. Taken September 2, 1979. Exposure not recorded, Kodachrome 64 slide film. The girl in front temporarily lost her balance and was almost swept away, but miraculously she recovered and made it across mostly dry!

Page 79. Sacramento River, California. Taken May, 1983. Exposure not recorded. In a scene reminiscent of Tom Sawyer and Huck Finn, Tim Palmer and I take off a couple days before our finals at Chico State University, build a raft, and float down the Sacramento river.

Page 82. Arua, Uganda. Taken October 31, 2005. F 3.2, 1/125th second, 82mm. Water from a tropical shower clings to a fragrant Plumeria flower (also known as a white frangipani).

Page 83. Stein Butte, Oregon. Taken June 6, 2004. F 3.2, 1/250th second, 67mm. On a rocky outcrop just a few feet below the summit of Stein Butte, a colorful display of Siskiyou Lewisia brings the colors of the circus to the great outdoors.

Page 84. Big Basin Redwood State Park, California. Taken August 14, 1980. Exposure not recorded, Kodachrome 64 slide film. Water droplets rest on a fern after a summer shower in the Redwood forest.
Page 84. Mt. McKinley Wilderness, Alaska. Taken August 8, 2004. F 3.2, 1/250th second, 75mm. California is known as the Golden State, and the state flower is the California poppy. But the golden flower is not limited to just California – here it graces a meadow as far north as Alaska.

Page 85. Sam's Valley, Oregon. Taken January 21, 2007. F 7.1, 1/160th second, 136mm. An oak tree rises above a snowy landscape to stand in silhouette against the early morning sunrise.

Page 86. Lower Table Rock, Oregon. Taken January 13, 2007. F 9, 1/250th second, 136mm. A white oak leaf is encased in ice in a vernal pool on the flat volcanic summit of Lower Table Rock.

Page 87. Upper Table Rock, Oregon. Taken January 19, 2007. F 8, 1/160th second, 45mm. A lone oak snag stands sentinel on the volcanic summit of Upper Table Rock. The shot was taken just minutes before sunset.

Page 88. Graves Creek, Galice, Oregon. Taken August 22, 2004. F 3.2, 1/125th second, 75mm. A late summer shower brings out the deceptive beauty in poison oak leaves which were just starting to turn a fall red.

Page 89. Murphy, Oregon. Taken November 23, 2006. F 13, 1/15th second, 180mm. Water droplets hang from Nandina berries after a rainshower. I went out to our garden to take some shots at different apertures in order to test the depth of field capability on a new lens I'd purchased, and this is one shot from the series.

Page 90. Whittier, Alaska. Taken August 8, 2004. F 3.2, 1/250th second, 75mm. A wild raspberry on a hillside in Alaska presented me with a dilemma: photograph it, or eat it? I think I proceeded in just that order!

Page 91. Big Basin Redwood State Park, California. Taken December 29, 1984. Exposure not recorded, Kodachrome 64 slide film. A red mushroom pushes up through the duff of a redwood forest.
Page 91. Lower Tent Meadow, Kings Canyon National Park, California. Taken July 30, 1979. Exposure not recorded, Kodachrome 64 slide film. I took this shot of a pinedrop at 6:30 a.m., just as the first rays of light started filtering through the forest.

Page 92. Arua, Uganda. Taken May 13, 2006. F 8, 1/160th second, 60mm. A clump of cactus creates interesting patterns in the afternoon light.

Page 93. Summit Lake, Elliot Creek Ridge, Oregon. Taken June 5, 2004. F 3.2, 1/350th second, 82mm. A bumblebee flits from flower to flower in a field of purple lupine.

Page 94. Murphy, Oregon. Taken March 14, 2005. F 3.2, 1/500th second, 75mm. Spring breaks forth as new blossoms on a flowering plum prepare to open.
Page 94. Summit Lake, Elliot Creek Ridge, Oregon. Taken June 5, 2004. F 3.2, 1/125th second, 75mm. The intricate design of a teasel is still visible long after the purple flower has died.

Page 95. China Creek Trail, Taylor Creek, Oregon. Taken May 25, 2006. F 8, 1/200th second, 85mm. A crop of new laurel leaves are born. The red leaves will soon turn green as they grow and mature.

Page 96. Palisade Point, Crater Lake, Oregon. Taken July 22, 2006. F 5, 1/200th second, 166mm. A whitebark pine grows from a rocky outcrop over the amazingly blue water of Crater Lake.

Page 97. Paradise Park, Mt. Hood. Taken August 5, 2006. F 8, 1/200th second, 152mm. Paradise Park is an apt name for the meadows on the west side of Mt. Hood. A plethora of wildflowers paint the hillside: Indian paintbrush, lupine, mountain aster, knotweed, yarrow, black eyed Susans, and many others.

Page 98. Epi Island, Vanuatu. Taken 2000. Exposure not recorded, Kodak 100 Gold film. A local Vanuatu girl showed my wife and kids how to use a taro leaf as an umbrella when caught in a sudden tropical downpour!
Page 98. Below Johnson Peak, Kings Canyon National Park, California. Taken August, 1980. Exposure not recorded, Kodachrome slide film. In a moment of frivolity, Urban Faubion climbs inside a whitebark pine snag and strikes a gnarled tree pose!

Page 99. Laurel Creek Canyon, Kings Canyon National Park, California. Taken June, 1981. Exposure not recorded, Kodachrome slide film. Helen takes a ride on a make-believe unicorn in an enchanted forest of whitebark pine snags.

Page 102. Zermatt, Switzerland. Taken April, 1990. Exposure not recorded, Kodachrome 64 slide film. The moonscape and earthscape are eerily similar as the last rays of sun highlight a snowy ridge next to the Matterhorn.

Page 103. Mt. Hood from Dollar Lake, Oregon. Taken August 3, 2006. F 5, 1/80th second, 85mm. A half moon peeks out from behind the north face of Mt. Hood as the last rays of alpenglow light the summit.

Page 104. Stein Butte, Oregon. Taken October 6, 2006. F 10, 1/8th second, 216mm. I spent a night on top of Stein Butte and the highlight was watching a full moon rise over the Siskiyous in the east as the sun set in the west.

Page 105. Silver Lake, California. Taken December 29, 1982. Exposure not recorded, Kodachrome 64 slide film. A group of us camped by Silver Lake and took advantage of the light of the rising full moon for a night ski.

Page 106. Fish Lake and Mt. McLoughlin, Oregon. Taken September 7, 2007. F 8, 35 minutes, 19mm. The shot was taken facing the North Star on a clear night with no moon. The whitish tint on the right side of the photo is the Milky Way galaxy.
Page 106. Helix Nebula (NGC7293). Taken August 15, 2007. 1 hour exposure finishing at 2:57 a.m.. I took the shot at the observatory at New Hope Christian School using a 16" Ritchey-Chrétien reflector telescope. David Bowdoin helped me set up the telescope and post process the image.

Page 107. Eagle Nebula (M16). Taken August 15, 2007. 1 hour exposure finishing at 12:30 a.m.. Once again the shot was taken at the observatory at New Hope Christian School, and David Bowdoin helped me set up the 16" reflecting telescope and post process the image.

Page 108. M109 galaxy. Taken April 12, 2007. 20 minutes. I took this shot of the M109 galaxy at the observatory at New Hope Christian School. David Bowdoin helped me set up the 16" reflecting telescope and John Bunyan helped me post process the image.

Page 109. Sawtooth Peak, Sequoia National Park, California. Taken June 30, 1979. Exposure not recorded, Kodachrome 64 slide film. David Houghton contemplates the sunset from the top of Sawtooth Peak, where a group of us from Sierra Mountaineering Experience spent the night.

Page 112. Harris Beach State Park, Brookings, Oregon. Taken April 1, 2006. F 10, 1/320th second, 216mm. This Western Grebe was at the edge of the incoming tide and made no attempt to move away as I took pictures, approaching closer and closer until I was only a few feet away. He didn't appear injured, and when we returned from a walk down the beach he was gone.

Page 113. Harris Beach State Park, Brookings, Oregon. Taken March 25, 2006. F 5, 1/500th second, 317mm. The seagulls at Harris Beach State Park must get a lot of handouts from those who picnic there, because they are quite fearless. This one let me approach to within ten feet.

Page 114. Merlin, Oregon. Taken February 3, 2007. F 7.1, 1/400th second, 448mm. An African Augar Buzzard at the Wildlife Images animal rehabilitation center. This bird came from Mozambique and is one of the highest flying birds in the world, soaring along on huge wings at altitudes of over 17,000 feet.

Page 115. Entebbe, Uganda. Taken August 20, 2006. F 5, 1/250th second, 320mm. The Crowne Crane is Uganda's national bird. This one was wandering free around a zoo in Entebbe.

Page 116. Merlin, Oregon. Taken February 5, 2007. F 4.5, 1/250th second, 320mm. A Bald Eagle at Wildlife Images, which is a rehabilitation center for injured wildlife. 80% percent of the animals brought to the center are later released back into the wild.
Page 116. Applegate Valley, Oregon. Taken April 1, 2007. F 5.6, 1/400th second, 320mm. A Black Swan is silhouetted against a reflection of a cloudy sky as raindrops gently ripple the surface of the pond.

Page 117. Ashland, Oregon. Taken April 28, 2007. F 4, 1/400th second, 320mm. This Wood Duck was in Upper Duck Pond in Lithia park, and I clicked the shutter just as he glided through a reflection of the evening sun striking the pink blossoms of a tree at the pond's edge.

Page 118. Entebbe, Uganda. Taken August 20, 2006. F 5, 1/250th second, 288mm. The intricate detail and patterns in a peacock's tail feathers caught my eye. The peacock was wandering free around a zoo in Entebbe, Uganda.

Page 119. Crescent City, California. Taken November 26, 2006. F 4, 1/320th second, 195mm. A California sea lion at the Ocean World aquarium stops to pose for a photo. The handlers allowed me to remain by the tank after the official tour, and I got a number of candid shots.

Page 120. Efate, Vanuatu. Taken 2002. Exposure not recorded. My son Kevin carefully navigates his way through a jellyfish bloom. Literally thousands of jellyfish filled the water, and swimming through them without getting stung was an adventure at which we were only partly successful!

Page 121. Top left, Purr-fect Pets, Grants Pass, Oregon. Taken April 10, 2007. F 5.6, 1/100th second, 136mm, studio flash. Other three, dentist office, Medford Mall, Oregon. Taken April 3, 2007, all at 80mm with available light. I found that getting good photos of tropical fish in aquariums is more difficult than it appears: there isn't much light, the fish are small and constantly on the move, backgrounds can be distracting, and external flashes often reflect off the glass of the tank in unexpected ways.

Page 122. Vibora, Bolivia. Taken August 1983. Exposure not recorded, Kodachrome 64 slide film. The landing gear on the New Tribes Mission plane I was on broke when we touched down on the jungle airstrip. A South American Mission plane is here seen in the background bringing in spare parts so our plane could be repaired.

Page 123. Santa Anita, Bolivia. Taken September, 1983. Exposure not recorded, Kodachrome 64 slide film. This quiet stretch of river in the Amazon River basin provided a surprise for me when I reeled in my hand line. The stingray weighed over 60 pounds!

Page 126. Strawberry Peak, California. Taken March, 1982. Exposure not recorded, Kodachrome 64 slide film. I was out for a cross country ski in the arid mountains above Los Angeles when a white dog befriended me and accompanied me on my ski outing. He seemed to relish the white powder as much as I did!

Page 127. Williams, Oregon. Taken May 27, 2006. F 6.3, 1/160th second, 180mm. Jasmine, my daughter's thoroughbred horse, gallops across a meadow to rejoin her filly.

Page 128. Entebbe, Uganda. Taken February 4, 2006. F 11, 1/400th second, 200mm. Two white rhinoceros feign sleep in the hot afternoon sun.

Page 129. Murchison Falls State Park, Uganda. Taken July 4, 2004. F 6.3, 1/500th second, 238mm. A giraffe's vantage over the African plain makes it impossible to sneak up on him.

Page 129. Entebbe, Uganda. Taken August 20, 2006. F 5, 1/320th second, 254mm. A mother vervet monkey calls out to another monkey as her baby beneath her nurses.

Page 130. Glastonbury, Connecticut. Taken June 24, 2007. F 5, 1/200th second, 232mm. A squirrel rummages in the grass under a bird feeder to see if he can scare up anything to eat.

Page 131. Applegate River, Oregon. Taken June 13, 2005. F 4.5, 1/350th second, 75mm. A swallowtail butterfly is backlit along the shore of the Applegate River. In the summer, our family often goes down to the river to swim, fish or read. And of course I can't resist stalking the butterflies, to see how close I can get to them with my camera.

Page 132. Merlin, Oregon. Taken February 5, 2007. F 4, 1/125th second, 320mm. A female grizzly bear at Wildlife Images takes a stroll shortly before entering a time of hibernation.

Page 133. Murchison Falls State Park, Uganda. Taken March 10, 2007. F 7.1, 1/500th second, 320mm. An antelope is poised to run on the open plain. His body faces in one direction and his head in another, perhaps to confuse potential prey about which way he will run. My friend who was driving the Land Rover leaned back so I could take the shot through his open window. After I clicked the shutter, the antelope took off, but I forget if he went right or left!

Page 134. Merlin, Oregon. Taken February 5, 2007. F 4, 1/250th second, 174mm. A bobcat pads along on silent paws at Wildlife Images.

Page 135. Murchison Falls State Park, Uganda. Taken March 11, 2007. F 5.6, 1/320th second, 254mm. A herd of elephants are accompanied by several black birds, who eat the insects that fly off the ground when the elephants move. There are actually five elephants in the photo – you can just make out the two babies who try to stay hidden behind their mothers.

Page 136. Chasm Lake, Kings Canyon National Park, California. Taken August 4, 1979. Exposure not recorded, Kodachrome 64 slide film. An inquisitive yellow-bellied marmot takes a pause from eating roots to give me a once over as I slithered toward him on my stomach. Getting close-ups of wildlife in the days when I only owned a 50mm lens was indeed a challenge!

Page 137. Mt. Goddard, Kings Canyon National Park, California. Taken August 6, 1979. Exposure not recorded, Kodachrome 64 slide film. Sleeping on top of 13,568 ft. Mt. Goddard was a fitting culmination to an 11 day solo backpacking trip. Setting up my bright red tarp on the summit was a challenge, but thankfully the clouds started to disperse at sunset and I didn't get wet.

Page 141. Arua, Uganda. Taken May 14, 2006. F 6.3, 1/100th second, 45mm. A group of boys along a dirt road in Uganda loved having their picture taken, and they would squeal with delight upon seeing themselves on the LCD screen. Just as I was about to take this picture, the guy in the middle ran up and craned his neck so that he could also be in the photo. There are a lot of eyes in the photo, but the whites of his eyes became the central focal point.

Page 142. Williams, Oregon. Taken July 13, 2006. F 7.1, 1/320th second, 150mm. My daughter Nika's love for horses is evidenced in this shot with Princess, a three-month-old filly.

Page 143. Arua, Uganda. Taken August 31, 2006. F 5, 1/60th second, 75mm. The arresting stares of the children on a dirt road in rural Uganda testify to both their poverty and their hope.

Page 144. Miller Lake, Oregon. Taken June 25, 2006. F 5.6, 1/125th second, 216mm. Early morning backlight helps emphasize my son Kevin's cast as my wife enjoys the peaceful quiet of the mountain lake.

Page 145. Arua, Uganda. Taken May 7, 2005. F 3.2, 1/60th second, 159mm. A Bible translator from the Omi language of the Democratic Republic of Congo checks out the pictures in a *National Geographic* issue which focused on polar bears – an animal never before seen in that part of the world!

Page 146. Battle Rock Wavefinding Point, Port Orford, Oregon. Taken October 17, 2006. F 16, 1/640th second, 70mm. My wife and I take an early morning stroll down the beach. I took the shot using a tripod and a self timer, and we ran so that we would be at just the right place when the shutter released.

Page 147. Arua, Uganda. Taken May 14, 2005. F 7.1, 1/100th second, 48mm. A group of boys in rural Uganda take a break from picking and eating wild mushrooms to pose for a picture.

Page 148. Isiro, Democratic Republic of Congo. Taken November 2, 2003. F 4.7, 1/760th second, 108mm. Due to the civil war in the Congo, the roads have fallen into disrepair, and bicycles are the principal means of transporting goods. Here a man takes home a load of firewood for his cooking fire as the sky behind him turns purple with an approaching tropical storm.

Page 148. La Cruz, Bolivia. Taken November, 1983. Exposure not recorded, Kodachrome 64 slide film. The lines in the old woman's face and the simple stitching in her old dress give silent witness of how difficult life can be.

Page 149. Ashland, Oregon. Taken November 4, 2006. F 5.6, 1/60th second, 174mm. Matt and Lea Matters happily vow to spend the rest of their lives loving each other and loving God.

Page 150. Pistol River State Park, Oregon. Taken November 27, 2005. F 3.2, 1/500th second, 67mm. My son Kevin launches off the edge of a sand dune over an expanse of virgin sand that seems to just beg for his footprints!

Page 150. Epi Island, Vanuatu. Taken 2002. Exposure not recorded, Kodak 100 Gold film. My daughter Nika finds a pair of nautilus shells on a remote beach in the South Pacific.

Page 151. Riverside Park, Grants Pass, Oregon. Taken July 2, 2006. F 5.6, 1/125th second, 216mm. Each summer a number of churches in Grants Pass join together for a "Church in the Park" service. Worshipping God in the outdoors is a new and wonderful experience for many of those who attend.

Page 152. Diembering, Senegal. Taken 1995. Exposure not recorded, Kodak 100 Gold film. My wife holds the daughter of our house helper, who named her after my wife – Laura.

Page 153. Diembering, Senegal. Taken May 19, 2000. Exposure not recorded, Kodak 100 Gold film. Myself with our kids departing from the village of Diembering for the last time after having finished the translation of the Kwatay New Testament. Within the hour a rebel fired on our truck with an automatic weapon. Photo taken by my wife Laura.

Page 158. Crater Lake, Oregon. Taken January 22, 2007. F 11, 1/200th second, 320mm. The cliffs rising above the water in Crater Lake are reflected amongst a thin layer of skim ice, broken up by several small islands along the edge of Wizard Island. The ice, which had formed in several places during the cold night, melted not long after I took this photo from the crater's rim.

Page 159. Middle and North Sister from Golden Lake, Oregon. Taken August 8, 2007. F 8, 1/200th second, 61mm. Middle and North Sister are reflected in the rippled surface of the lake just after the sun set.

Page 160. Mt. Brewer and Brewer Lake, Sequoia National Park, California. Taken August, 1980. Exposure not recorded, Kodachrome 64 slide film. The alpenglow on Mt. Brewer is reflected amongst icebergs in Brewer Lake.

Page 160. Ridge Lake, Emigrant Wilderness, California. Taken August 9, 2005. F 3.2, 1/90th second, 59mm. The cliffs of Granite Dome are reflected in a meadow tarn near Ridge Lake. At 9,500 feet, there is just a short time each year when the ground is free of snow, and so the growing season for wildflowers and corn lilies is very short.

Page 163. Damariscotta Lake, Maine. Taken June 26, 2007. F 8, 1/250th second, 208mm. A golden sunrise filters through the trees and hits steam rising off the lake. The shot was taken at 5:30 a.m. I was glad the camera was on a tripod, because I was busy swatting mosquitoes as I clicked the shutter!

Page 164. South Sister from Camp Lake, Oregon. Taken August 7, 2007. F 7.1, 1/125th second, 56mm. Early morning light hits South Sister and the meadow at Camp Lake. The red volcanic rock and the white snow lend a splash of color to the blue lake and green meadow.

Page 165. Green Lake, Whistler, British Columbia. Taken July 14, 2005. F 3.2, 1/250th second, 59mm. I went out into the frosty air before sunrise to take pictures, and was following a black bear around a golf course when I noticed this beautiful reflection on the lake.

Page 166. Harris Beach State Park, Oregon. Taken November 25, 2006. F 11, 1/500th second, 184mm. My son Kevin takes a moment to praise his God for the wonder and beauty of all he has created.

Page 176. Heceta Head, Brookings, Oregon. Taken October 16, 2006 by Laura Payne. F 3.2, 1/180th second, 82mm. My wife Laura and I went over to the Oregon Coast for our 19th anniversary, and although it rained almost the entire weekend, there were a couple short breaks when we could enjoy the views. Laura took this shot of me after we had finished photographing the lighthouse on Heceta Head in the background.

Back cover. Crater Lake, Oregon. Taken May 12, 2007. F 5, various shutter speeds, 19mm. I skied up and slept on top of The Watchman at the edge of Crater Lake and woke up to take this panorama of the sunrise at 5:50 a.m. The photo is composed of three shots taken with a wide-angle lens on a tripod, and each of the shots were exposed three times using auto-exposure bracketing, and then combined using the High Dynamic Range (HDR) software package Photomatix.

To purchase a fine-art print of any of the photographs in this book,
please visit www.TheCreatorsCanvas.com

About the Author

STEPHEN PAYNE attended Multnomah Bible College from 1984-1986. He majored in Bible, minored in missions, and was photo editor of the student newspaper. Since 1987, he and his wife Laura have served with Wycliffe Bible Translators. After translating the New Testament into the Kwatay language of Senegal, Steve worked as a translation consultant in Vanuatu, New Caledonia, the Democratic Republic of Congo and Sudan. The Paynes currently live in Grants Pass, Oregon, with their two children Nika and Kevin. Steve works for The Seed Company – an affiliate of Wycliffe Bible Translators – making trips overseas to train mother tongue translators and translation consultants in French speaking Africa. Steve has been an avid photographer for 30 years, winning several awards and photographing five different continents. He is also an avid hiker and has done extensive hiking and climbing around the world, and has been a guide for several mountaineering organizations.